Teaching of Science

for

Primary and Secondary
Pre and In-Service Teachers

Rajinder M. Kalra
Former Dean (Academic) NIE, NCERT; Former Summer Faculty (2004) (Science Education-Elementary), Simon Fraser University, Burnaby, BC, Canada; Professor Emeritus, International Institute of Adult and Life Long Education, Delhi

SHIPRA

(Reprinted also, First Published 2003)

Rs 995

ISBN: 978-93-91978-87-7

2025 Imp. PoD

Teaching of Science

Published by:
SHIPRA PUBLICATIONS
LG 18-19, Pankaj Central Market
I.P. Ext., Patparganj, Delhi 110092, India
91 11 47322068; 9650028065, 9810522367
info@shiprapublication.com
www.shiprapublication.com

Preface

It is gratifying to note that some significant changes in our school curriculum have been made especially at the elementary level. It is also worth mentioning that emphasis is being given to in-service orientation programmes for practising teachers especially at the elementary level in India. But, more importance is to be placed on qualitative rather than quantitative aspect of these in-service programmes for practising teachers. Effective planning, monitoring and evaluation of in-service education programmes are somewhat missing. These programmes are generally conducted in a mechanical manner. Sometimes the participants of these in-service programmes opine that the transaction during these orientation programme is nothing but a condensed pre-service training programme. Lack of relevance and vitality of the in-service programmes is another drawback which needs careful consideration. The resource faculty of these programmes in majority of cases, use "talk and chalk" (lecture) method and thus fail to impress upon the usefulness and applicability of modern methods of teaching in actual classroom situations.

It is truly said that teachers should be taught what they are supposed to teach. Therefore, the in-service education programmes at the elementary level should be directly proportional to elementary school curriculum. Thus, methodologies, innovations, transaction of new elementary school curriculum may be included in these in-service programmes which these participating practising teachers are required to follow in their actual classroom teaching situations. Furthermore, these new strategies need to be practised in these in-service orientation programmes in simulated classroom situations. Thus, the participating in-service teachers, in general, should be acquainted with modern teaching-learning devices. Emphasis should be placed on development of competencies in the teachers which have direct bearing on inculcating the same in their pupils. Due importance and meaningful linkages between pre-service and in-service education programmes may be established. To give importance and to fulfill the above convictions, it may be imperative to organise in-service programmes for teacher educators at the elementary teachers training institutes as the techniques of teaching at the elementary level are different and sometimes more difficult than secondary level teaching. This is one of the major weaknesses of the elementary education in majority of the developing countries.

Coming to the specifics of meaningful science education for in-service teachers, it may be imperative to make these teachers realise that to be a modem dynamic elementary school teacher, one may have to be involved in developing new methods of teaching-learning and devise new strategies for transacting the recent innovations in science education at the elementary level. Thus, these participating teachers must practice these modern teaching-learning strategies with special reference to environmental studies and science education (at the primary and upper primary levels) in these orientation programmes. Simulated classroom, outside classroom situations, may be arranged to accomplish these objectives.

The author in this academic venture has made some efforts to achieve the above mentioned objectives. He contends that no matter what is put in print to ensure that an orientation programme based on competency approach and in the context of MLL for in-service teacher, will be executed in such a way as to de-emphasis straight memorisation and emphasis understanding the context of real problem. If the in-service teacher does not sympathise with this approach, the orientation programmes for practising teachers will be no better than the formal pre-service teacher education programme. There is an impression that in-service training is just a ritual to cross the EB (Efficiency Bar). The most important contribution of the elementary school teacher must be his/her ability to make interpretations, innovations, invent his/her own study units and make them come to life by adapting to opportunities in living environment.

Let us think, organise and strive together as professional teachers so that our pupils can discover for themselves the value of logical enquiry, institution and the general process of innovations for both themselves and their community.

I must extend my thanks to teachers and perspective teachers for their response to the first edition of this book. In this second enlarged edition one more chapter 'Introduction to Science' is added for the benefit of its readers.

Rajinder M. Kalra

Contents

I

Introduction to Science

> Believe nothing merely because you have been told it; or because you yourself have imagined it; do not believe what your teacher tells you, merely out of respect for the teacher; but whatever after due examination and analysis. You find to be conclusive to be the good, the benefit, the welfare of all beings, that doctrine believe and cling to, and take it as your guide. —*Lord Gautam Budha*

The following deliberations concerning the concept of science and its nature of learning science is an outcome of author's teaching at Canadian Universities and abroad. These convictions have been summarized by taking into convictions of international science educators concerning science.

What is Science?

- Science is a systematized knowledge of our environment.
- Science is man's systematic investigation of his environment.
- Albert Einstein "The whole of science is nothing more than a refinement of everyday thinking".
- Science involves describing, predicting and explaining nature and its changes in the simplest way possible.

Basic Activities of Science

(i) To accumulate information through observations.
(ii) To organize this information to seek regularities in it.
(iii) To wonder why the regularities exist.
(iv) To communicate the findings to others.

All science is built upon the results of experiments. The discovery of regularities permits simplification of observation.

Who is Scientist?

A scientist does not have to be Ph.D. or M.Sc. in Chemistry, Physics, Biology or Astronomy.

Fable: A lost child in a summer camp loses his way, dark and cold. He wants to keep himself warm. He decides to keep himself warm and gather material for a fire.

Will Burn	*Won't Burn*
Tree Limbs	Rocks
Brooms	Black Berries
Dry Leaves	Marbles

He strikes stones to have fire and burns the twigs to keep himself warm.

The organisation of information was quite an aid to keep himself warm. He is acting as a scientist.

Scientists ask questions, make predictions based on scientific concepts, design and conduct experiments to obtain experimental answers.

Science and Technology—Its relationship

Science is the study of natural world with the goals of describing, explaining and predicting substance and changes. The goal of science is to develop or test a scientific concept. Science is essentially research (an intellectual pursuit). Concept start as hypothesis and end as discarded or accepted theories of law.

Technology is the skills, processes and equipment required to manufacture useful products or to perform useful tasks. Technology is an activity that runs parallel to science. As scientific knowledge increases, the number of instances of technology as applied science increases.

Technology, glassware, battery, the laser and computer technologies and scientific concepts are created by people and used by people. Science and technology are interrelated and inter-dependent.

Science Skills and Processes

1	2	3	4	5	6
Observing	Measuring	Classifying	Inferring	Predicting	Communicating

7	8	9	10	11
Hypothesis	Designing experiments	Controlling variables	Interpreting data	Formulating models

Observing—obtaining information about object, situations or events.

Measurement—non standard and standard units. Length, Area, Volume, Mass, Time-intervals and Force are among the measurements and units in metric systems.

Classifying—grouping objects, concepts or events on the basis of observable properties, similarities and differences.

Inferences—based on observed data and past experience.

Predicting—a forecast is made about future events on the basis of observed data, extrapolation.

Communicating—process of organizing and processing data that occurs between the observation stage, and interpretation or generalization stage.

Hypothesizing—'educated guess' made about an expected relationship between two variables to explain a cause and effect relationship. A hypothesis should be testable.

In order to learn about science in depth, it is imperative to know about the nature of science learning.

Nature of Science Learning

- Young children love doing science. Science is doing.
- The nature of science includes development of active inquiry, critical thinking, independent work, understanding the world of science incorporating understanding from different perspectives such as art, music, poetry, story telling, social sciences, math. Science is defined as systematic knowledge of our environment.

Who is Excellent Science Teacher?

Passion	Caring	Reflection	Understanding (of the subject matter)
(Passionate about learning, teaching and working with children)	(Caring for and about children)	(Reflecting on one's own teaching and on children's learning)	To much knowledge of particular area of science can create problems when you try to implement a child centered, inquiry based classroom

Pillars of Successful Science Teaching

The following are five pillars of science teaching:

1. Do not underestimate your students.
2. Do not be misled by students first reaction to your question. "I don't know"! Rephrase the question. No supplying fix answer.
3. Children construct their own knowledge and meaning. Children make connections and construct knowledge based on their personal experiences, previous knowledge, emotions, value, aesthetics, beliefs etc.
4. Let children take control over their learning. Children learn by mistakes. Evaluate what went wrong and why. Not too much teacher talk and teacher dominating their work.
5. The key to a successful classroom is to create atmosphere in building community of young scientists.

Teaching is not a profession where you can take a recipe and implement it in the classroom. Every classroom and every child is different.

Critical thinking involves being open to new ideas (open minded) but at the same time being skeptical. Many aspects of critical thinking are: (i) Questioning the accuracy of particular statements. (ii) Examining what is and is not relevant to a particular problem. (iii) Identifying the ambiguity of particular statements. (iv) Detecting biases. (v) Identifying underlying assumptions.

Goals of Science Programme

The following are some goals of effective science programmes:

(i) To develop an understanding of the nature of science which include, designing, conducting experiments or observational studies and evaluation.

(ii) Students should be involved in "talking" science. This process includes the social skills of conducting talks, listening and communicating effectively.

(iii) Students should be engaged in inquiry.

(iv) Students should construct through and elaborate understanding of science concepts.

(v) Students should develop integrated understanding of various phenomena. (Artists, poets, historians and mathematics may have different ways of understanding).

(vi) Respect for our environment, understanding of patterns and relationships in the environment.

(vii) To nurture curiosity.

(viii) To learn how to observe and communicate.

(ix) To encourage questioning, analytical and critical thinking.

(x) To nurture independent learning and thinking.

(xi) To help students make connections between different perspectives.

(xii) To help students evaluate the appropriateness of different perspectives (such as science, art, social and other cultural conceptual contexts).

(xiii) To develop an enthusiasm and interest in science.

II

Teaching Learning Environment at the Elementary Level in the Developing Countries

The developing countries are required to catch up with the developed world. This is because the world has become interdependent, and no country can live in isolation. This implies designing of models of accelerated progress by the developing countries which emphasises assimilation of the past, mastery of the present and perspective thrust for future especially relating to national development.

Development does not mean merely economic development but it also includes development of inner qualities of man and quality of life. In this context, education has a major role to play. Education that promotes quality of life, motivation of action and productivity, and optimum utilisation of scarce resources is ideal for development.

In order to operationalise such educational programme, teachers will have to develop new methods of teaching and learning. They will have to devise new curricula and new programmes of education. The developing countries will have the problems of developing a new climate of scientific and technological progress, and at the same time they will have to preserve their own cultural identity. This has pedagogical implications emphasizing among children development of the powers of observation, experimentation and invention. At the same time, students will have to absorb the lessons of history and culture in a living manner so that the accumulated wisdom of their culture becomes a vibrant force in the life of the school and the community. Keeping in view the above, the role of the elementary school teachers needs to be refined.

Three Important Elements in Elementary Teaching

1. Encouragement for participatory teaching learning process in such a way that every child gets opportunity to actively interact with the teacher and with the classmates.
2. Promotion of creative activities in classroom in such a manner that students are encouraged to express themselves through writing and art activities.
3. Promotion of collective activities of children in such a way that children develop team spirit, collective co-operation and productive project work.

Competencies to be Developed

In order to achieve the above, the following competencies are required to be developed in the prospective and practising (in-service) teachers by the elementary teachers training institutions and other concerned institutions dealing with education in the developing countries.

1. Competence to understand the right process of learning, including learning to learn, learning by doing, learning to be, learning to do and learning to become.
2. Competence to devise dynamic methods in the day to day situations based on the needs and interests of children.
3. Competence to organise the classroom in such a manner that different kinds of activities may be organised in it so that children may receive required guidance from the teacher.
4. Competence to become an example of the qualities that he/she wants to develop among his/her students, realising that example is superior to mere instruction and preaching.
5. Competence in regard to language, delivery of speech and other methods of communication.
6. Competence in regard to the contents of the subject that he/she is supposed to teach. The teacher should be able to answer questions that belong to the immediate lesson or even to some remotely related subject matter which may occur in subsequent lessons.

7. Competence to engage children in a dialogue in a meaningful manner so that children may develop capacity to ask questions and may be inspired to find out the answers by themselves.

8. Competence to innovate so as to create proper environment in the classroom to enable children to develop wider horizons of perception.

9. Competence to develop among students a scientific temper which is often confined to cultivation of mere attitude of questioning. Scientific temper also includes objective observation, experimentation and consideration of every point of view relevant to the enquiry in a logical manner.

The competencies mentioned above suggest that the contemporary elementary school teacher in the developing countries may inspire a change in the impulses of the pupils growing personality so as to have a balanced blending of knowledge, power, love and skills that are required for his/her development as a good individual and useful member of the society. The teacher has to develop competencies to innovate methods of teaching which are learner oriented and learner's need based. The teachers may be apprised what they are supposed to teach.

Recent Developments in Elementary Education in India

It is gratifying to note that the Government of India, has undertaken a challenging task of improving the quality of primary education under the District Primary Education Programme (DPEP). In the planning process of DPEP, ample scope has been provided to have a meaningful feedback about various pedagogical and management conceptual activities which have been developed over a period of time. DPEP stresses on decentralisation (role of Panchayat and Village Education Committees), Girls and Women's Education, Non-Formal Education, Teacher Education, Nutritional support to Primary Education, Distance Education and Adult Literacy. Adequate emphasis has been given on in-service training at the elementary level.

Minimum Levels of Learning

The National Policy on Education has stressed on laying down Minimum Levels of Learning (MLL's) for each class or grade at the elementary level in terms of performance goals including competencies to be developed in students, more meaningful and focussed approach to the educational process at the elementary level. These NPE imperatives, especially mentioned under DPEP have ramifications on in-service teacher educational programmes for elementary school teachers.

In-service Training of Teachers

In-service training of teachers is a basic component of life long education. The purpose of in-service training of teachers is to meet the changing requirements of education system, teachers and other educational personnel, to improve the standard of teaching and thereby improving the quality of the education system. Earlier in-service training of teachers was considered as an input to enhance professional standard and continuation of their pre-service training.

The thirty-sixth session of the International Conference on Education (Geneva, 1977) advocated in-service training of teachers as the right of teachers for their information needs.

In-service training organisational methods may vary in different countries but there is agreement and keen interest in finding an appropriate, relevant and operational form of in-service training of teachers. The following action points may be taken into consideration while initiating an in-service training of teachers.

1. Identification of teachers' needs and problems related to actual classroom teacher.
2. Planning of in-service programme in advance.
3. Selection of suitable resource persons.
4. Utilisation of modern education technological devices emphasising multi-media approach.
5. Utilising 'school complex' concept for the in-service education programme.
6. Conducting a massive programme for teachers.

7. Evaluation and follow-up of in-service education as an inbuilt component of the total programme.
8. Use of mobile units of in-service education programme for rural and remote areas.
9. Providing financial/professional incentives for participating in-service teachers. These include steps such as in-service training may be linked with promotion, and a credit system may be introduced for participation in in-service teacher education programmes. It was felt that a comprehensive scheme for in-service training needs to be developed.

Conclusion

To conclude, one may reasonably infer that no educational improvement can take place unless the quality of teacher is improved. Investment in improving teacher education system, especially at the in-service level, can yield rich dividends in the light of financial resource inputs *vis-à-vis* financial investment required. In this venture, the author has made an attempt to provide meaningful and relevant science education experiences (along with innovating strategies) to the practising teachers at the elementary level. It is worth mentioning here that there has been quantitative expansion of in-service training programmes but qualitative aspects of these programmes need substantial improvement. The real quality and effectiveness of these training programmes is demonstrated by their impact on actual classroom teaching situations. This also requires "Administrative" and "Sincere Will" for improving quality of education.

III

Curriculum Development in Science Education
Based on Competence Approach

> If science is to be pursued with full vigour and zest and is to become a mighty force in the Indian renaissance, it must derive its nourishment from our cultural and spiritual heritage. Science must become an integral part of our cultural fabric. It is possible that when science takes root in native soil, and is no longer an exotic plant, its growth pattern may be visibly influenced by those features which have been characteristic of Indian philosophic thought and civilisation. *—Education Commission (1964-66)*

We are living in an atomic, space and IT age where students are bound to be concerned with some fundamentals of science and their applications in everyday living. This applies not only to students but to all youth living at home, in the community and in the school. The vast scientific knowledge which can help in these syndromes does exist and is available in books and publications. There are numerous scientific magazines and journals reporting research being conducted in various parts of the world. But an avalanche in scientific knowledge has thundered down upon man in the last few years.

The teacher in a school must be aware of the subject matter which he/she must teach within the prescribed time period in an academic year. There are many problems faced by a teacher.

- How does he/she include all the knowledge, resulting from this explosion in scientific knowledge, within the textbooks?
- What today's student studying elementary science is supposed to learn?
- What are they actually learning?

- What does the study of science contribute to student's educational development besides facts, concepts and generalisations? Any skills? Any values?

The answers to the above questions depend upon the existing curriculum in schools and teacher training institutions. To respond to the above, it may be imperative to discuss the historical perspective of curriculum development in science education at international and national levels:

Curriculum Developments in Science Education: International Perspective

The major developments in science education resulted from the "Psychic Shock" of "Sputnik" (in 1957) suffered by the western scientific community. This forced them to re-examine their attitude towards the curriculum of science for their schools.

Almost overnight AAAS, ESEC, ESSP, CMESP, H.O.S. became the major new alphabet soup of American Elementary Science Education. PSSC, BSCS and the CHEM study were the science education programmes at the secondary level in 1960's. Massive financial support from the National Science Foundation and similar agencies transformed the face of American Science Education. "Discovery", "Investigation", and "Enquiry" suddenly became the key words in science education programme. Recently concept mapping for meaningful learning science became another major contribution in the field of science education. In U.K., Nuffield programmes in science education were developed and implemented. At the elementary level, the major programmes, such as University of Illinois Elementary School Science, Robert Karplus and Associates in the University of California Elementary School Science Project, Elementary Science Study, Water Town Massachusetts and recent Hands on Science (HOS) Programme (1988) were developed. A brief description of the elementary science education programme is as follows:

University of Illinois Science Project

The Elementary Science Education Curriculum was developed by a staff of professional astronomers and educators from the University of Illinois. The major objective of this programme was to present a new organisation of elementary school science content based on identification of fundamental concepts and principles that incorporate in a given scientific field. Each of their books was tested with elementary school children and revised wherever necessary.

University of California Science Project

Robert Karplus, a physicist, developed an elementary science education programme based on scientific literacy. His own definition of scientific literacy required students to develop "sufficient knowledge and experience so that they will be able to have some understanding of scientific work being carried out by others even though they themselves do not become scientists". The major thrust in this elementary science programme was on teaching pupils to look at natural phenomena from the scientific point of view, encompassing a scientific conceptual framework and language.

Elementary Science Study Project

The work of the Elementary Science Study proposed a new coherence in the elementary science curriculum and suggested that objectives of teaching-learning of science, assimilated in the earliest years, can be effectively related to many other disciplines during the earliest school years.

Some units of elementary science study were developed during the 1962 Summer Conference at the Newton South High School, Newton, Massachusetts. The following units were developed in these areas : Micro-ecology, plant growth, laboratory science, elementary physics, charges and currents, gases and airs, animal coloration, cell unit, astronomy, animal behaviour and locomotion, geology, physics and light, and psychology of learning. In addition to these units, texts, graphic materials, apparatus and teacher aids were devised.

Concept Mapping for Meaningful Science Learning

Joseph Novak *et. al.*, an originator of this strategy of science learning describes a concept map as a schematic device for representing a set of concept meanings embedded in a framework of proportions. Concept maps present a brief schematic of what has been learned.

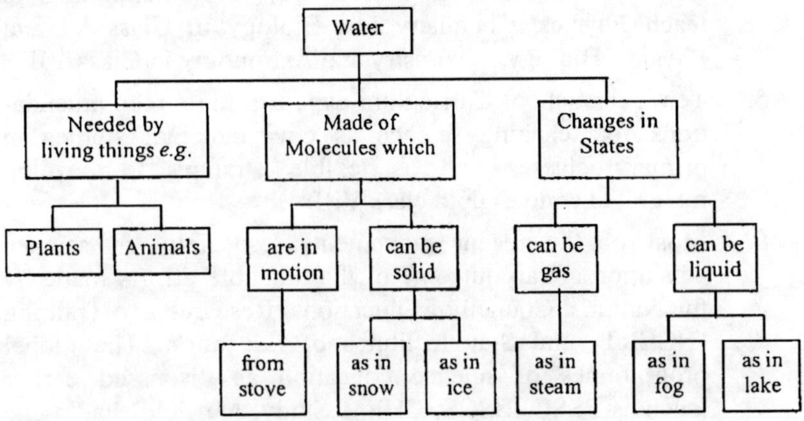

Figure 1—A concept map for water showing some related concepts and propositions.

To summarise, concept mapping is a strategy/technique for externalising concepts and propositions which is one of the most important components of Integrated Science teaching.

Curriculum Developments in Science Education in India—An Overview

After independence, laudable efforts have been made concerning improvement of education in general and science education in particular. Numerous commissions and international agencies made the following general recommendations concerning science education in India:

1. The University Grants Commission's recommendations for teaching of science from primary school to the completion of undergraduate classes.
2. The Secondary Education Commission's recommendations for introducing certain broad aspects of science *i.e.*, General Science at the middle school stage and high school stage.

3. UNESCO Planning Missions recommendations for teaching Biology, Physics and Chemistry in classes VII and VIII as an integral subject.
4. Education Commission's (1964-66) recommendations to teach Physics, Chemistry and Biology in Class VI and Physics, Biology, Chemistry and Astronomy in Class VII.
5. Ten Year School Curriculum expert group's recommendations for teaching science as environmental studies in primary classes and a flexible strategy to develop integrated courses upto class VIII.
6. Most of the recent movements, especially in science education are an outcome of the laudable efforts made by the National Council of Educational Research and Training (NCERT) and State Institutes of Education. The global programmes of science education as discussed earlier (such as PSSC, BSCS, CHEM Study, Nuffield) had some impact on the curriculum development programmes in science education in India. Integrated Science Education Curriculum and Environment at Science may be considered as one of the major improvements in existing science curricula.

Inspite of the above developments in science education, it is not very encouraging to note the observations (which seem to be justified) made by Dr. Sethna, Ex-Chairman, Atomic Energy Commission.

> "Over the years there have been a large number of conferences on science education and yet science education has not improved noticeably and in some respects one might say that it has deteriorated."

The above contention of Dr. Sethna has been substantiated by Razario and Gupta (1978) suggesting to the "accepted fact that state of science teaching in our country is highly unsatisfactory", observed that one of the major facts in "science teaching in rural areas, is the wide communication gap between the urban planners of school science curricula and the conditions prevailing in rural schools and common curriculum is designed for urban and rural students without taking into consideration the latter's environment."

After a decade, some improvements have been made in the field of science education. Today, India stands on the threshold of nuclear energy. If our country is to benefit fully from this powerful tool for progress, we must find a way to change our attitude towards science education.

Science in democratic societies benefits all people and we must ensure that they become aware of the advantages which science can bring to their lives.

Yashpal Committee Report (1993) suggested that text should give analytical reflection of real life situations.

The efforts made for improvement of science education under:

1. The Hoshangabad science curriculum,
2. Eklavya Science Activities and
3. Kishore Bharti Teaching Learning Material in Science Education at the elementary level are laudable and praiseworthy.

Recently, "Science for All" has become the slogan of science educators around the world. This was an outcome of the programmes of the American Association for the Advancement of Science (AAAS-1985). "Project 2001, Science for All Americans" became another alphabet in American Science Education.

In mid eighties, another movement Science, Technology and Society (STS) became a significant approach in science education which emphasized that science, technology and society are inter related: Yager (1984) became the proponent of this approach: Denis W. Cheek (1992) provides an overview of STS approach. This approach suggests application of science and technology in improving living standards which may respond to a sense of social responsibility of science education. It is based on student's needs, interests with optimum utilisation of local resources. AIDS and Drugs prevention have become another area of concern in school education.

Minimum Levels of Learning

National Council of Educational Research and Training (NCERT), in collaboration with Ministry of Human Resource Development

(MHRD), has developed Minimum Levels of Learning at the elementary level in India.

It is gratifying to note that the National Policy on Education (1986) has laid stress on science education in school education. It also emphasized the need for achieving Minimum Levels of Learning (MLLs) in different school subjects at each stage of school education. This may help teachers in organising meaningful teaching learning experiences and evaluating pupil performances. The basic features of MLL include relevance and functionality, achieveability, understandability and evaluability.

Science at the primary stage is taught as Environmental Studies (EVS). EVS is classified into two separate curricular sub-sections, *viz.*, Social Studies and Science usually referred as EVS Part I and EVS Part II. Under EVS (Classes I and II), holistic approach for teaching science and social studies is implemented and science is not introduced formally. Beyond Class II, the split approach (Science and Social Studies) is implemented.

The following ten major competencies are to be developed in a pupil at the primary level under Minimum Levels of Learning in Environmental Studies (1995).

The Pupil

1. Acquires awareness about one's well-being in the context of social and natural environment.
2. Explores important aspects of one's socio-civic environment and comprehends their working.
3. Knows about various people at work and appreciates the importance about the 'world of work'.
4. Understands and interprets the spatial and interactive relationship between man and his environment.
5. Begins to see the relationship between man's past and present, and to hold the past in its proper perspective.
6. Senses common but simple and easily observable socio-economic situations and problems, analyses them and seeks possible solutions at his level of experience.

7. Understands the factors contributing to the preservation of good health.
8. Develops skill in gathering and classifying information about living things from the environment, and drawing simple inferences.
9. Observes and examines some common characteristics of non-living things.
10. Observes simple phenomena on the earth and in the sky and draws inferences.

At the upper primary level Classes (VI to VIII), the following units have to be dealt with.

Class-VI

1. Science in Everyday Life
2. Things around us
3. Separation of Substances
4. Measurement
5. Changes around us
6. Motion, Force and Machines
7. The Living World
8. Structures and Functions of Living Things
9. Air-I
10. Water
11. Energy-I
12. Balance in Nature
13. The Universe

Class-VII

1. Nature and Composition of Substances
2. Acids, Bases and Salts
3. Heat
4. Light
5. Sound
6. Electricity

7. Energy-II
8. Organisation of the Living Body
9. Water-II
10. Air-II
11. Life Processes
12. Food, Health and Diseases
13. Soil
14. Agricultural Practices and Implements

Class-VIII

1. Carbon and its Compounds
2. Energy Crisis/Alternative Sources of Energy
3. Metals and Minerals
4. Man made Materials
5. Atom and Atomic Energy
6. Pressure
7. Light and Optical Instruments
8. Magnetism
9. The Microbial World
10. Electric Current
11. Adaptation and Organic Evolution
12. Useful Plants and Animals
13. Conservation of Natural Resources

To provide meaningful teaching learning experience concerning Minimum Levels of Learning (MLLs) at the primary level and open competence level at the upper primary level, the preceding Chapter III has been developed for the pupils and presented as an exemplary unit.

IV

Teaching of Science at the Elementary Level *Based on Competency Approach*

To help pupils solve real life problems, to process adequately the explosion of scientific knowledge (information processing) and to think creatively, fostering and nurturing of the concept of "Open Competence" in a learner is of prime importance.

Components of "Open Competence" Approach to Elementary Science Education Programme: An Overview

1	2	3	4	5	6
Process skills (Scientific Methods)	Comprehension of fundamentals of Science (as against memorisation)	Science as a way of thinking	Development of scientific attitude, temperature and habits	Science and values	Science and citizenry

Components of "Open Competence" Approach

The concept of open competence in development of an elementary science programme, especially for teacher educators, may include the following components.

1. Process Skills

These skills or scientific methods include:

1. Observation.
2. Formulating hypothesis.
3. Designing experiments.
4. Measurement, Recording.

5. Inference.
6. Generalisation.
7. Formulating models.

2. *Comprehension of Fundamentals of Science*

More emphasis should be given on comprehension of fundamentals of science as against memorisation. This implies that a basic aim of science teaching, especially at the elementary level, is to supply foundational knowledge of science which may be brought into use in the daily environment through study and application of science. This may also provide a systematic, practical and balanced view of the discipline of science to change students' behaviour through their knowledge. A holistic view of science is imperative to present "Balanced Science for All" which may include the following :

1. Concepts in Science,
2. Processes of Science,
3. Social and Cultural aspects of Science,
4. Moral and Ethical aspects of Science.

3. *Science as a Way of Thinking*

The teaching of science at the elementary level may encourage permeation of the spirit of science as a way of thinking. To accomplish this, one may take the help of the following approaches to scientific thinking:

1. Discovery/Inquiry/Investigation
2. Divergent and Convergent
3. Analytic and Synthetic
4. Imaginative and Creative

4. *Development of Scientific Attitudes, Temper and Habits*

Science teachers all over the world have long recognised that proper scientific attitudes are among the important outcomes of meaningful teaching learning situations.

The writer contends that the development of scientific attitudes could be demonstrated as the ability to do the following:

1. To view facts objectively.
2. To be free from dogma and superstitions.
3. To revise one's opinion as evidence warrants.
4. To have a spirit of inquiry.
5. To be open minded.

Success in developing scientific attitudes depends ultimately on the teachers, and it is important that the science teacher should always keep in mind that pupils form attitudes more from examples than from abstract precepts. In the third world countries especially, rural people and pupils have certain superstitions about diet, astrology, patent medicine, self-doctoring and the like that should be dealt with when the pupils reveal them.

5. *Science and Values*

There is a great danger in science as a singular value system, for if the weakness of various ethnic cultures in the third world countries is their resistance to scientific thinking, there has been an equal stubbornness on the part of Western scientific culture in its over-commitment to technology. The above conviction was aptly described by the Education Commission India (1964-66) in the following paragraph:

> If science is to be pursued with full vigour and zest and is to become a mighty force in the Indian renaissance, it must derive its nourishment from our cultural and spiritual heritage. Science must become an integral part of our cultural fabric. It is possible that when science takes root in our native soil and is no longer an exotic plant, its growth pattern may be visibly influenced by the features which have been characteristic of Indian philosophic thought and civilisation.

Teaching Learning Strategies in the Open Competence Approach

The following are some teaching learning strategies which may help in the 'open competence' approach to science education at the elementary level in terms of MLLs.

1. Acquisition and development of knowledge, skills, attitudes, and values relevant to a wide variety of local environmental activities.
2. Fundamental of scientific concepts, with an open attitude towards science, relating to a wide variety of situations.
3. Activities involving divergent and convergent thinking.
4. Creativity.
5. Information storage and processing.
6. Problem solving.
7. Transfer of learning from one situation to another.
8. Ability to cope with new challenges concerning socio-economic changes.
9. Application of knowledge to real-life situations.
10. Capabilities to catch up with possible changes.
11. Values clarification.
12. Analysis and synthesis of knowledge.
13. Science teaching-learning encouraging innovations.

The open competence approach from the operational point of view may be summarised in the following categories :

1. Informatics (Information Storage and Processing)
2. Application of knowledge in practical life (Problem Solving)
3. Curriculum to have sufficient alternatives so that the teacher has both attitude and responsibility for making curriculum changes.
4. Creativity in science education at the elementary level.
5. Science based on environmental needs.
6. Science education to meet individual differences.
7. Decision making.

1. *Informatics*

The 21st century is the 'Information Age'. We are living in an atomic and space age where our young students are bound to be concerned with some fundamentals of science and their applications in everyday living. The elementary school teacher may have to face many problems while teaching science. How does he include all the information resulting from this explosion in scientific knowledge within the textbooks?

2. *Application of Knowledge in Practical Life Problem Solving*

The Problem-solving approach suggests application of knowledge in practical life which is action-oriented.

3. *Curriculum to provide Sufficient Alternatives and Teacher Involvement in Curriculum Development*

It is gratifying to note that the old doctrine that the teacher should not have any say in curriculum development, is being challenged in some of the third world countries.

Many organisations should contribute to the curriculum development, but in the ultimate analysis, unless the teacher understands, believes in, is ready for, and accepts some responsibility for a change in curriculum, the change will be in name only. There should be wide use of advisory committees comprising, for example, retired teachers, local community members who have sound science education ideas, and others who are concerned with local needs but who at the same time are aware of national interests.

Finally, science curriculum development is a dynamic process and must never be static. Also, the science curriculum at the elementary stage should have sufficient alternatives so that the teacher has both the latitude and responsibility for making curriculum changes.

Thus, the science curriculum at the elementary stage should always be in a process of revision leading to modernisation, reinforcement and enrichment.

4. *Creativity in Science Education at the Elementary Level*

One of the most satisfying experiences an elementary school teacher can have is to see 'the gleam of desire to learn' in the eyes of a highly motivated student. Intelligent and pointed questions which show that a student really cares about science or any school subject, is the response every elementary school teacher desires.

To motivate students, who have the capacity to work, an activity which is creative and challenging is required.

Development of creative genius of students is one of the most important objectives in the educational process. The elementary school teachers, especially those teaching science, have a great responsibility to the nation to ensure that teaching of science encourages creativity potential in a child and results in the making of a "creative person".

Obsurn defines a creative person as:

> One who perceives and imagines hidden relations and has the impulse to incorporate them in material form so that the others may perceive them also. Such people can and do frame in their constructive imagination poems, paintings, sonnets, and symphonies that have never been perceived.

Dr. Paul Torrance states about creativity in the following paragraph:

> I have chosen to define creative thinking as the process of sensing gaps or discerning missing elements, forming ideas or hypotheses concerning them; Testing these hypotheses; and communicating the results, possibly modifying and re-testing the hypotheses. The creative child produces something new, original, at least to himself and stresses divergent thinking rather than convergent one.

The above discussion on creativity or creative thinking may be summarised in the following four broad areas:

1. It is new and novel, different from the existing ideas and oriented towards the values of society.
2. It is diversified in approach, format and practice.
3. It requires intense motivation
4. It is a special type of problem-solving.

5. *Science Education based on Environmental Needs*

Totally different system of science education is needed to enable students to develop skills and acquire knowledge which may help them to produce better way of life for themselves, their families and their communities based on their local environment. A new curriculum in science education, which may be called "Environmental Science Education", needs to encourage the students to find themselves the ability to discover knowledge for themselves, everyday problems of the environment and applying same for problem solving.

6. *Science Education to meet Individual Differences*

Science education, especially at the elementary level, must be in accordance with the philosophy of continuous growth progress. We may design an individualised programme of instruction in science education. Our instructions system may take cognizance of the student to be appreciated for what he is and for what he has the potential to become.

The National Policy on Education (1986) emphasise the concept of a Child Centred Approach in the following words:

A warm, welcoming and encouraging approach, in which all concerned share a solicitude for the needs of the child is the best motivation for the child to attend school and learn. A child-centred and activity-based process of learning should be adopted at the primary stage. First generation learners should be allowed to set their own pace.

IIlich (1971) emphasises the importance of individual differences and suggests that our educational system may enable the learners to become more self-directed and self-responsible.

7. *Decision Making*

The explosion in scientific and technological knowledge has increased the importance and relevance of decision making competencies in the students. It may involve values clarification, identification of alternatives for action, and recognising the consequences of each alternative in terms of priorities of the national goals.

V

Recent Approaches to Teaching Learning Science

"If you can't fly, then run.
If you can't run, then walk.
If you can't walk, then crawl.
But whatever you do, keep moving —*Martin Luther King*

For many years there has been a need for curriculum improvement especially in science education at the elementary level in India. The elementary school teacher, because of his own educational background and the curriculum load that is brought to bear on him, places almost total emphasis on memorisation of certain facts and principles of science just to pass the class examination even though understanding of the concept memorised may generally be lacking. Elementary school teachers tend to teach as they were taught; descriptive and addictive methods are prevalent.

Considering these aspects of the environment for the teaching and learning of science that prevail in some elementary schools, especially in rural areas, one wonders what might be done to the nature of the elementary science education to bring about a desirable change in this existing situation.

In the opinion of this writer, different approaches to science education which may encourage the students to find in themselves the ability to discover knowledge and develop skills which may help them to produce a better way of life for themselves, their families and their communities. To achieve the above objective, one has to bring a drastic change in pre-service elementary teacher education curriculum along with an effective in-service teacher education programme especially in imparting meaningful science education experiences at the elementary level.

To provide effective science education experiences at the elementary level, it may be imperative to discuss recent trends and approaches to teaching learning science in the in-service teacher education programme. These recent approaches may include:

1. Environmental Education: an Introspection;
2. Science, Values and Applications to daily life environment; and
3. Integrated Approach to science teaching.

Environmental Education—An Introspection[1]

Man's life is closely related to the environment on the earth. This environment consists of two major elements-biological and physical environment. The biological environment refers to the food obtained by plants and animals, while the physical environment *i.e.*, land, water and air provide favourable conditions for existence and growth of different forms of life, including man.

Awareness of the environment always existed in mankind and man has been awed by its mysterious and beautiful magnificence. The Indo-Aryans used to live amidst the splendour and majesty of nature which left an everlasting effect on them. In the Pre-*Vedic* period, they were greatly inspired by the magnificent aspects of nature and sung hymns to nature. *Varuna*, the God of the water; *Mitra*, the Sun; *Prithvi*, the Earth; and *Agni,* the fire, '*Soma*' and others. These were the *Supreme Beings* who were worshipped with great faith since early Aryan history. The *Rigveda* consists of instructions on rituals, songs and verses on nature.

Nature is now considered a continuous process. Change is a natural phenomenon in nature. The changes which may be gradual or abrupt are basically for establishing an overall balance or equilibrium if we consider the earth as a whole.

Man has been using environmental resources since times immemorial to meet his ever increasing needs for a better living. But unfortunately, man has failed to acknowledge the fact that he can receive from the earth and atmosphere only so much as he gives to it. He has crossed the limits of nature's vast abundance and has eventually caused serious disturbances in the ecological and environmental balance. According to this balance, the relative numbers of organisms or natural resources in a particular environment remain constant. If this balance is disturbed, everything coming under the environment is affected; there is a shortage of food for various organisms. Floods are caused by deforestation, extinction of various flora and fauna etc. Human activities such as indiscreet disposal of waste products (that of agricultural and industrial chemicals, garbage etc., lead to water pollution) and toxic fumes from automobiles, industries etc., cause extensive air pollution.

The natural environment of man is therefore to be viewed in its totality. It can be better understood and appreciated if the interaction between its various components is carefully observed and studied which calls for Environmental Education (EE).

The study of environment, as a separate identity, that is, environmental education came up in the seventies. In the past there have been school systems of different countries, such as Nature Study, Field Study, Outdoor Education etc., which stressed on EE. But in these observations or activities, nature has been considered in isolation with no connection whatsoever with other aspects of life.

Only on realisation that man was also a part of the environment, did the whole attitude towards Environmental Education change. Gradually, many people have recognised the role of Environment in our lives and due to this sincere public response, Environmental Education has found its way into the school curriculum.

What is Environmental Education?

Environmental Education consists of an integral education which lasts throughout life continuing through all formal and non-formal stages. It is the process of clearing notions and acknowledging values in order to develop attitudes necessary to become aware of the inter-relationship between man, his culture and his biophysical environment. EE stresses on the complexity of environmental problems and considers the environmental aspects in plans for development and growth. It enables the discovery of the root causes of environmental problems and provides the attitudes and knowledge required to play a constructive role in the improvement of life and values.

The United States Environmental Education Act (1970) has symbolised this movement:

> "For the purposes of this Act, the term *environmental education* means the educational process dealing with

> man's relationship with his natural and man-made surroundings, and includes the relation of population, pollution, resource allocation and depletion, conservation transportation, technology, and urban and rural planning to the total human environment".

Environmental Education provides an insight into the inter-dependence of economy and ecology among different countries and the need for everyone to unite. By examining the major environmental issues at all levels, local, national, regional and international—the students also get an idea of the environmental conditions in other geographical areas. Environmental Education provides the basis for a new international establishment which ensures improvement and conservation of the environment.

Environmental Education can provide an extremely important contribution in the restricting of educational systems by involving individuals in problem solving process and providing them with responsibility and commitment to build a better tomorrow. According to the International Union for the Conservation of Nature and Natural Resources Commission of Education International Working Meeting on Environmental Education in the School Curriculum, Paris, UNESCO (1970), Environmental Education can be defined as follows:

> Environmental Education is the process of recognising values and clarifying concepts in order to develop skills and attitudes necessary to understand and appreciate the inter-relatedness among man, his culture and his biophysical surroundings. Environmental Education also entails practice in decision-making and self formulation of a code of behaviour about issues concerning environmental quality.

Thus, Environmental Education is integration of different disciplines and educational experiences which enables more rational and judicious actions to be taken, which takes into consideration the relation of socio-economic development and improvement of environment and are capable of meeting social needs.

The objectives of the Environmental Education programme as established in the agreement brought about between UNESCO and UNEP are as follows:

1. To facilitate the co-ordination, joint planning and pre-programming of activities essential for the development of an international programme in Environmental Education.
2. To promote the international exchange of ideas and information pertaining to Environmental Education.
3. To co-ordinate research to better understand the various phenomena involved in environmental teaching and learning to design and evaluate new methods, curricular materials and programmes, both in school and out of school (youth and adult) in Environmental Education.
4. To train and retrain personnel to adequately staff the Environmental Education programme; and
5. To provide advisory services in Environmental Education to Member States.

Conceptual Models of the Environmental Education Curriculum

There is a controversy about whether to refer Environmental Education as an 'approach' or a 'discipline'. If it is not considered as a 'discipline' then it loses its status of sufficient identification to be incorporated into a curriculum. But on the other hand, considering it to be a 'discipline', then its character of 'totality' or 'integration' is lost.

Thus, to solve this problem, two conceptual models of Environmental Education curriculum have been drawn up.

1. Interdisciplinary or infused model
2. Multidisciplinary or infusion model

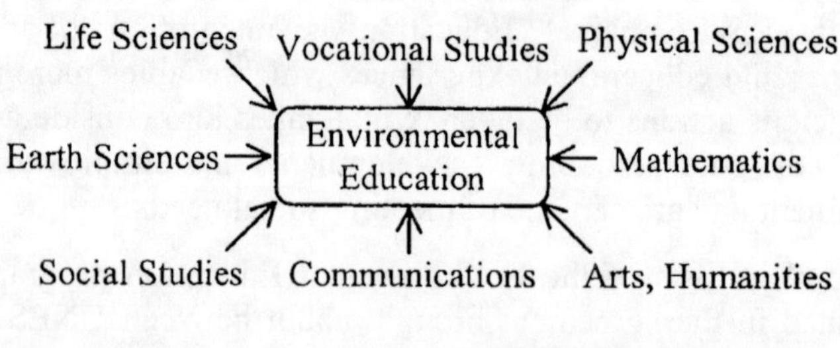

Figure: Interdisciplinary (Infused Model)

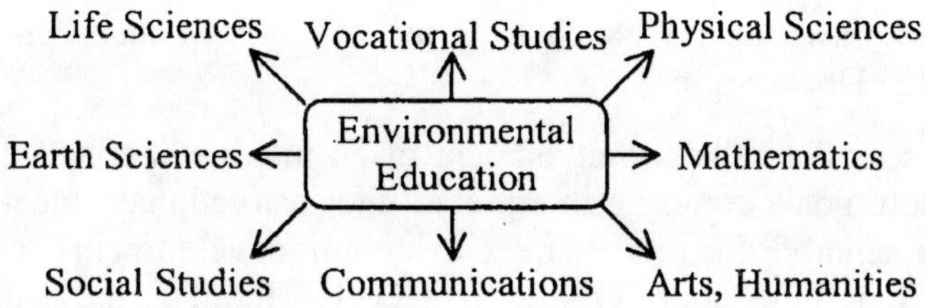

Figure: Multidisciplinary (Infusion) Model

Source: UNESCO, Strategies for Developing an Environmental Education Curriculum, Paris, Unesco (1980)

Goals and Objectives of Environmental Education

Goal setting is very important and useful. Schools, large or small, should keep these in mind while making decisions concerning Environmental Education.

The goals of Environmental Education are:

1. To promote an awareness and sensitivity about social, economic, political, ecological interrelationship in rural and urban areas.
2. To enable every person to acquire skills, attitudes and knowledge required for protection and improvement of the environment.
3. To recreate the whole attitude of individuals, groups and society as a whole towards the betterment of environment.

Objectives of environmental education are:

1. Awareness of environmental problems.
2. Knowledge and understanding of the problems faced.
3. Attitudes developed which commit the individuals or society for betterment of the environment.
4. Skills to identify and solve problems.
5. Participation of various social groups and individuals.

The problem is how to interpret these goals and objectives for developing an effective curriculum in Environmental Studies. To resolve this problem, a model Environmental Education curriculum has been drawn up for North America which is in accordance with the Tbilisi Declaration.

This model calls for adjustment of an intermediate set of goals. Then these goals could be interpreted into instructional objectives of Environmental Education. The curriculum development goals are categorised into four grades or levels, though they are not necessarily limited to a particular level. For instance, certain ideas or concepts of Level II could be used in Level IV.

These goals are consistent with the Tbilisi Declaration and are very important in curriculum development. They involve a step by step development of knowledge, skills and attitudes, where the contents are taught according to increasing maturity. Here follows a brief introduction of the levels and the associated goals:

Level I—This focusses on the basic ecology. It is the 'Knowledge level' and helps in making decisions which are rational and are in accordance with the environment.

Level II—At this level, concepts are developed. Even this is the 'Knowledge level', but concerning the behaviours of human beings in connection with the environment. These concepts evolve around activities affecting the environment.

Level III—This is a 'skill level' which emphasises those skills that are required for issue evaluation, investigation and clarification of values.

Level IV—This level is concerned with the 'training and application' of the skills required for maintaining an equilibrium between the quality of life and environment.

Thus, these goals provide a basis for development of a comprehensive curriculum, which consists of the ecological principles and consequences of man's activities.

A sound Environmental Education curriculum must have a multidisciplinary approach in which no particular discipline is dominant and leads to an interdisciplinary relationship.

Now, a decision needs to be made *i.e.*, which model should we select for incorporating Environmental Education into our present day school curriculum. For resolution of this problem, the following conceptual model Modified/adapted version of model for Environmental Education has been suggested by UNESCO (Strategies for developing an Environmental Education Curriculum; Paris, UNESCO, 1980) with special reference to Elementary Education.

Elementary Level

Primary (5 years)		*Upper Primary (3 years)*	
Level I			
Ecological foundations	Environmental Problems Environmental studies	Ecological Community	Languages, Social Science
Level II			
Conceptual awareness	Art Environmental Science Mathematics Languages	Conceptual framework Social, Cultural, Economic and Environmental make up	Mathematics, Experience
Level III			
Investigation and Elementary Action Skills	Health and Physical Education	Investigation and Evaluation conceptual, Attitudinal development	Art Education Health and Physical Education

The model shows how the scope can be infused through grade levels (vertical organisation) and across the apt disciplines (horizontal organisation).

Scope refers to the total breadth of the curriculum in a subject field.

Sequence deals with the question of the placement of curriculum materials from the standpoint of time.

Environmental Education in the National Curriculum Framework

India has been using the environment as a foundation for learning since a long time, but it is only in the recent past that environmental concepts and components have been incorporated formally into the school curricula.

In 1963, the country's syllabus of General Science from Classes I-VIII was environment based and distributed into specific areas like housing, clothing, shelter, air, weather and water etc. Emphasis was laid on acquiring knowledge and skills about the environment through strategies using the pupils immediate environment.

According to the recommendations of the Education Commission (1964-66).

> The aims of teaching science in the primary school should be to develop proper understanding of the main facts, concepts, principles and processes in the physical and biological environment.

Minimum Levels of Learning and Environmental Studies at the Elementary Level

"Environmental Studies" approach is based upon the child's organised investigation of his own immediate surrounding. This approach may lead to a progressive development of skills, attitudes and concepts. It aims at developing the child's interest in his own immediate environment and then to go beyond his own immediate surroundings and experiences.

To evaluate "Environment studies" component at the primary stage, one has to lay down Minimum Levels of Learning (MMLs) in terms of competencies which may serve as performance goals for students and teachers in the total educational scenario at the elementary level. These competencies to be developed in this approach are related to cognitive, effective and psychomotor domain. Furthermore, these should be operationally feasible, relevant and in consonance with the experiences of the children and may identify 'hard spots' of teaching-learning process. Hopefully, this may lead to mastery level of learning in addition to continuity in learning in an integrated manner.

To summarise, one may suggest that in Classes I and II, the accent should be on cleanliness, formation of healthy habits and development of the power of observation. These should be emphasised again in Classes III and IV, but the study should include personal hygiene and sanitation. The child may also be introduced to the formal areas of science such as the plants and animals in his surroundings, the air he breathes, the water he drinks, the weather that affects his daily life, the earth he lives on, the simple machines that are being used in his environment, the body of which we should take care and the heavenly bodies he looks on at night.

At the Upper Primary Stage (Classes VI-VIII)

"...environmental activities will lead to the study of natural and physical sciences, history, geography and civics; constructive and creative skills will provide the basis for the practice of simple arts and crafts; and the practice of healthy living will serve as the foundation for physical education..."

Thus the aim of Environmental Education in elementary schools should focus on the development in students of ability to work with the materials in their environment and some problems as close to reality as possible. Thus general objectives should lay emphasis on performance rather than on accumulation of facts.

Evaluation in Environmental Studies

Evaluation consists of three main components:

1. collecting information,
2. forming judgements about whatever collected,
3. making educational decisions based on these judgements.

Evaluation of EE is a bit different from other disciplines as it is not a single 'discipline', but interdisciplinary in nature. There are other unique features like long term results, problem focussed approach, and community oriented attitudes which affect the evaluation system. An adequate evaluation model must incorporate these characters. The evaluation system should pay emphasis on understanding rather than memorisation. For this goal to be achieved, attempts should be made to combine evaluation of the pupil, curriculum and programme and show their interdependence.

Some Suggestions for Evaluation System in Environmental Education

These suggestions are desirable and should not be considered as prescriptive; nor are they necessarily applicable to all situations.

1. For evaluation in EE, stress should be put on helping pupils learn to think to create new combinations from the existing data. That is to say, evaluation should, itself, be an act of teaching.
2. Evaluation in EE should not be confined within the school building. Field trips should be an integral part of the school programme. The students should be encouraged to utilise community facilities.
3. Another important aspect to be kept in mind is that students should be given opportunities to develop the concept of self evaluation. They should be encouraged to participate in group discussions and try to see their strengths and weaknesses, and develop their own values and attitudes about issues.
4. The broad aim of environmental studies should be to develop in students the ability to work with the materials of their environment and to solve problems presented to them.

Limitations and Difficulties in Implementation of Environmental Education

Some of the problems envisaged in implementation of EE are as follows:

1. Lack of motivation.
2. Lack of knowledge about global aspect.
3. Values conflicts.
4. Capacity of learners.
5. Lack of supplementary and reference materials.
6. Lack of time for teachers for planning of activities.
7. Completion of syllabus and time constraint.
8. Lack of administrative support.

The practising teacher may discuss practical strategies in overcoming the above difficulties and limitations to provide meaningful experiences to our pupils at the elementary level. One of the possible strategies for achieving this objective is to teach science with a focus on values and applications of the same to daily life environment of students. This approach also envisages the concept of integrated science at the different levels of school education. The above mentioned strategies and approaches are being discussed.

Science, Values and Applications to Daily Life Environment

The author, through his experience and contacts with educators in India, believes that the new curricula in science education offer far from satisfactory solutions to the problems of teaching science to our students. While these newer curricula may go a long way to filling the needs of the above average students, it appears that something further is needed to meet the needs of average and below average students.

What, then, should be the nature of science education for our students?

Basically, a totally new system of science education is needed that will enable young students to develop skills and acquire knowledge which has a higher probability of producing a better understanding of their environment, and which will make possible for the students in acquaintance with the process of discovery of knowledge. Such a curriculum in science would not lay emphasis on theoretical and scientific principles that are unrelated to the students daily life. The emphasis would be placed on the application of scientific knowledge, improvement of living conditions, and certain other aspects of everyday life.

Philosophy and Aims of Science Teaching

A philosophy of science teaching consists of aims and objectives of teaching in general and of teaching of science in particular. For this reason, a science teacher needs some understanding of educational philosophy. The objectives are derived from the philosophy. The objectives of science teaching may be classified into categories which are different in scope. The kind of science education advocated for our students in the schools by this writer is described as follows.

The first aim of science teaching is that the students shall demonstrate knowledge of the fundamentals of science. The basic aim of science teaching in the schools, especially at the upper primary level, must be to supply foundational knowledge of science which may be brought into use in daily life.

Thus, the main objective of the science teaching is to provide to the student a systematic and practical idea of the discipline of science and to change student's behaviour through this knowledge.

The second objective of science teaching is that students should demonstrate abilities which are the by-product of the knowledge. If the students have acquired scientific knowledge from science teaching, they consequently should develop abilities to behave scientifically. In order to achieve the above aim, the students should be able to locate, evaluate and generalise problems.

The third and most important aim of science teaching in elementary schools is to make the students into more alert citizens and better equipped to improve the community life. In order to achieve this aim, the course content in science should have practical applications to daily life. The relationship of science instruction to the school's attempt to help every individual lead a worthwhile life is admirably stated by Brunson and Dowling.

> A responsibility of the school is to help every individual to lead a worthwhile life. These situations which can be better met by an understanding of the basic concept of science become forts of science instruction. Physical and mental health which are affected by sleep, rest, fatigue, diet, exercise, posture and drugs can be assumed for the public. Self assurance, which comes from a sense of achievement and understanding of normal viability, is necessary to the best adjustment and can be built by the study of chemistry. Through an understanding of organic and inorganic changes, the pupil gains appreciations which help him to see himself in his proper place with relation to the world

about him. By constant practice in recognising problems, seeking evidence to be weighed and arriving at the conclusions, the scientific method becomes a basis for action with the pupil. Science can help present certain fundamental principles which should be understood through partaking in and preparing for home making[2].

The fourth aim of science teaching is that the students shall demonstrate knowledge of the contributions made by our Indian scientists in the modern world. In the opinion of this writer, an important thing for a science teacher to do in the elementary schools is to develop pride in the contributions made by Indian scientists in scientific literature. It is necessary for a science teacher to believe in the competence of Indian scientists. The teacher must stress their achievements in science in class so that students may develop pride in their scientifically rich heritage and consequently in themselves.

To summarise, a philosophy of this science teaching process is based on a new system of science education that will enable the students to develop skills and acquire knowledge which will produce better ways of life for them and which will make it possible to lead the students to the discovery of knowledge.

Thus, the science programme should be aimed at raising the level of scientific knowledge, skills and attitudes of the students to make them more productive in their home environments.

Science Teaching with a Focus on Values and Daily Life Environment

To accomplish the objectives mentioned above, science must be taught on four levels (refer to schematic representation No. 1); the facts level, the concept level, the values level, and the work-experience level.

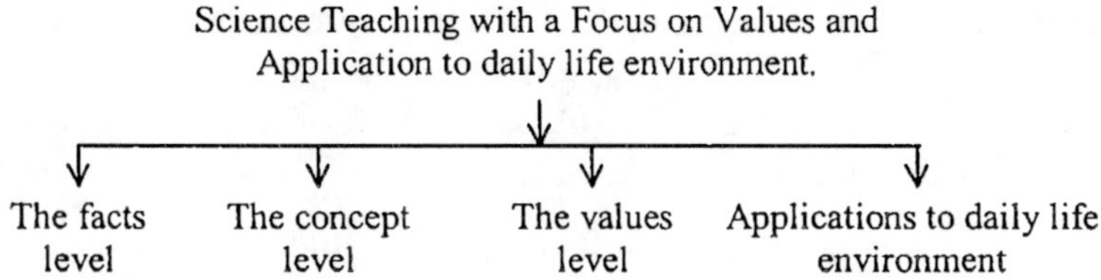

Innovations in Science Teaching

For example, in teaching a unit on water, the teacher might pose the following questions.

Water

Level I (Facts)

1. In how many physical states does water exist?
2. What are the common sources of water?
3. What are the methods of making water potable?
4. What are common solvents?
5. What is the chemical composition of water?

Activity I—Study plants in your farm. Find out how those plants should be watered in order to have maximum growth.

Activity II—Using a funnel, make some filtering beds with sand and gravel. Pour impure water containing mud in your locality. Find out how water gets cleaned after passing through the sand. Add alum to the water to kill bacteria.

Discuss with your parents if the above method can be used at home.

Activity III—If you are living on a farm, find out from your agriculture inspector how to check the purity of your own water supply.

Activity IV—How do the villagers select the location for digging of a well. What criteria do they use in deciding the best location for the well?

Activity V—If you are living in a city, visit a swimming pool where chlorine is being utilised. Investigate the method of transportation of chlorine and how much chlorine is needed in the water.

Level II (Concepts)

1. Demonstrate via certain lab experiments various methods employed in purifying water.

2. How do you know water is pure?
3. What are the effects of drinking impure water?
4. Demonstrate, via lab experiments, the chemical composition of water.

Level III (Values)

1. Why is water important to you?
2. What would you do without water?
3. Is the drinking water in your community fit for drinking?
4. If not, make a list of things you could do in your community to improve the quality of drinking water.
5. What action, if any, are you going to take along these lines?

Notice the emphasis on the "you" in each of the above values level questions (*Level III*). Although questions in *Levels I* and *II* may recognise applications, in today's world, they would not become *Level III* questions until they are directly related to the students' daily lives, environments and attitudes.

These "values" questions can be related to daily life environment.

Level IV (Application to Daily Life Environment)

Activity I—Investigate how water comes to your taps. Where does the water come from? How is it purified? (Refer to your local municipal water works engineer or technician for this activity).

Activity II—Study plants in your farm. Find out how those plants should be watered in order to have maximum growth.

Activity III—Using a funnel, make some filtering beds with sand and gravel. Pour impure water containing mud in your locality. Find out how water gets cleaned after passing through the sand. Add alum to the water to kill bacteria.

Discuss with your parents if the above method can be used at home.

Activity IV—If you are living on a farm, find out from your agriculture inspector how to check the purity of your own water supply.

Let us take another example in physics. This time the subject is the concept of machine which is commonly discused in science class.

Machines

Level I (Facts)

1. What is a lever?
2. How many kinds of levers are there?
3. Describe the simplest form of lever indicating the position of fulcrum, the resistance arm and effort arm.
4. What are simple machines?
5. How do we measure the work done by simple machines?
6. What are complex machines?

Level II (Concepts)

1. Draw diagrams of each type of lever showing the position of the fulcrum, effort and resistance.
2. One of the following items is not classified as a lever. Underline that item.
   (a) Screw, (b) Nut cracker, (c) Scissors, (d) Hammer.
3. Use a bar 10 feet long for the lever and a 20 pound weight for the resistance. Measure the effort with a spring balance and the distance with a metre rod.
4. Find out mechanical advantages for the following machines:
   (a) Wedge, (b) A wheel and axle.

Level III (Values)

1. How do levers help you in your daily life?
2. What machines do you use at home?

3. List all the simple machines you have at your house. Try to discover all the ways these machines could be used to help you do your work.
4. Make a list of some ways you could help others in your community learn to use simple machines.
5. Make a list of the advantages and disadvantages to be gained by using simple and complex machines to help you in your work.

Level IV (Applications to Daily Life Environment)

Activity I—Design some simple machines like a lever to make work easier at your farm and home (*e.g.*, block and tackle arrangement, wedges for splitting rock, wood, screws for lifting heavy loads).

Activity II—Study the following machines : (i) a sewing machine, and (ii) a printing press. Investigate how force is transmitted from one part of the machine to another. Also, study how the different parts of these machines are doing their jobs. (Visit to a printing press and sewing machine assembly plant would be quite helpful).

Activity III—Make a survey of pulleys which are commonly used in your community. Discuss various kinds of pulleys and their mechanical advantages.

Activity IV—Study the different kinds of hydraulic machines that are commonly available in your community. If a technician or an expert is available, get his help to explain the mechanism and operation of the above mentioned machines.

Activity V—Make a close study of a tractor. What simple machines and combinations are used in the above machines? Study the ways in which the simple machines have been assembled together.

Activity VI—Design a complex machine which is useful in your home by combining any two simple machines.

Here is an example, this time in the subject of food.

Our Food

Level I (Facts)

1. What is the chemical composition of the human body?
2. What is food made of?
3. What are the different food substances?
4. What are some common vitamins?
5. How is food digested?

Level II (Concepts)

1. Demonstrate via laboratory experiment that a living organism is made up of little divisions called cells.
2. What happens to the food you eat?
3. What is the importance of proteins in our food?
4. What are the advantages of a well balanced diet?
5. What is the result of a poor diet?
6. How do vitamins help our body?

Level III (Values)

1. Why do we eat?
2. Write a report containing two columns titled :
   (a) Food I Must Add to My Diet
   (b) Undesirable Foods I have Eaten
3. Make a list of the foods you have eaten during past two days and compare with the list of foods given in your textbooks. Are you getting enough vitamins?

Level IV (Applications to Daily Life environment)

Activity I—In certain parts of our country, the people eat only rice. What is lacking in their diet? What disease may result if this diet continues?

Make a study of eating habits of people in different States of our country. Write a report discussing deficiency in their diet suggesting ways to overcome the above problems.

Activity II—Test the presence of nutrients in your foods for proteins, sugar, fat and carbohydrate. Obtain the help from teacher or local doctor in this context.

Activity III—(Effect of food on the growth of rats). Take a pair of rats just weaned preferably from the same litter. Feed them some food *e.g.*, *roti*, carrot, water. To one rat, give an extra cup of milk a day. Weigh them regularly every three days. Record your results carefully and discuss in the class.

Transmission of Heat

Level I (Facts)

1. What do you understand by transmission of heat?
2. How does the transmission of heat take place in different substances?
3. Is there only one single method for transmission of heat in all the three states of matter?
4. Heat travels through liquids by convection, but not through solids, Why?
5. What is radiation?
6. How would you increase or decrease the rate of thermal conductivity?

Level II (Concepts)

1. Differentiate between good conductors and poor conductors of heat?
2. How can you prove that water is a poor conductor of heat?
3. How can you prove that iron is a good conductor and wood is a poor conductor of heat?
4. How would you find out whether copper is a good conductor or a poor conductor?
5. Why does more snow fall on high peaks of mountains?
6. How would you prove that black colour absorbs more heat?
7. What causes rain, dew and hail?

Level III (Values)

1. How would you protect yourself from heat if you are working near a furnace?
2. If you wear black or dark coloured clothes in summer, how would you feel?
3. Woollen clothes are generally coloured, why?
4. Handles of a pressure cooker are made of ebonite, why?
5. What is the importance of conduction of heat in your daily life?
6. How would you carry ice if you have to take it to a village from a city about 50 km. away?
7. Make a list of things you would need to make a thermos flask?
8. To what extent is it practical in India to copy European fashions in clothes?
9. If you are given two blankets weighing 2½ kg each or one blanket weighing 5 kg; which one should you take to keep yourself warmer?
10. What would you do to make your house cooler in summer and warmer in winter?
11. Where can you go in summer season to escape the heat?
12. Why are metallic pots preferred for cooking?
13. Why is the climate of sea-shore locations generally considered good for health?
14. Why is it warmer on plains than on higher altitudes?

Level IV (Applications to Daily Life environment)

Activity I—How would you prevent heat loss in your home through conduction and convection?

Make suggestions concerning the above problem.

Activity II—Try to devise the ways in which ventilation may make a room warmer instead of cooler.

Activity III—Collect different insulating materials which are used in construction of houses. Investigate the effectiveness of each insulative material to prevent heat loss.

Pump

Level I (Facts)

1. On what principle does a pump work?
2. How many types of pumps are there?
3. What are the different parts of a pump?

Level II (Concepts)

1. How would you prove that air is necessary for operating any pump?
2. What is the maximum depth from which water can be raised to ground level with a lift pump?
3. If depth is more than 30 feet, what kind of pump should be used?
4. Why cannot water be raised higher than 30 feet with a lift pump?
5. Why does not a water pump work well in summer?
6. Why does not a water pump work well in hilly areas?

Level III (Values)

1. What is the importance of water pumps in our life?
2. What are the advantages of a pump?
3. What changes would you make in a pump if you have to bring water to the second floor in your house?
4. If the water pump in your house does not work, how would you try to fix it?

Level IV (Work Experience)

Activity I—Set up a rubber plunger for cleaning a clogged pipe making use of air pressure.

Activity II—Construct a siphon and explain the working of your siphon with a demonstration. Discuss various conditions when the siphon would stop working.

Activity III—Write a letter to your Municipal Commissioner concerning water supply for your community.

Light

Level I (Facts)

1. What is light?
2. What happens when rays of light fall on any object?
3. What is reflection?
4. What is a lens? How many types of lenses are there?
5. How will you distinguish between a convex lens and a concave lens?
6. If two plane mirrors are bent at any angle then how many images will be formed of an object which is kept between these two mirrors?

Level II (Concept)

1. How will you prove that light is energy?
2. Which type of image is formed in a plane mirror?
3. If two plane mirrors are bent at an angle of 60° then how many images will be formed?

Level III (Values)

1. What colour of paint would you use in your room if you want to get more light in the room?
2. You are 6 feet tall and you want to see your full image in a mirror. What size of mirror would you buy?
3. What kind of a toy can you make using a plane mirror? Or how would you use a plain mirror to make a toy?
4. What type of mirror does a doctor use to examine your ear?
5. What kind of mirror is more practical for shaving?
6. What purpose does a side mirror serve in an automobile?

Level IV (Applications to Daily Life Environment)

Activity I—Make a list of the number of light bulbs which are used for lighting in your home, neighbourhood shops.

Find out in how many cases direct and indirect lighting is used.

Activity II—Write a report on the following topic?

Is your home and neighbourhood lighting satisfactory? If not, suggest some ways to improve lighting in your home and neighbourhood.

Also write a letter to the local Electricity Manager concerning unsatisfactory lighting in your home and neighbourhood.

The above levels, especially level IV (Application to daily life environment), suggest a detailed discussion on Environmental Education.

Integrated Science at Different Levels of School Education

Keeping the previous conviction regarding Science values and Applications to daily life environment, it is now easy to appreciate the importance of teaching and learning Science at school level. Three important questions arise in science teaching:

- What is to be taught?
- Why is it to be taught?
- To whom is it to be taught?

The answers to these questions will broadly cover all aspects of science teaching and its importance.

Jean Piaget has dwelt in detail giving his ideas relevant to science teaching and he has classified, on basis of age level of the pupils, the features of thinking and assimilating capacity. For simplicity purpose, we can classify the pupils on basis of their academic level into four categories, namely, primary level (upto V standard); Upper Primary level (upto VIII standard); Secondary level (Standard IX & X) and Senior Secondary level (Standard XI & XII). It is now established and accepted that science is studied in integrated form upto X and then it branches off into specialised fields like Physics, Chemistry etc., from XI Class.

Learning of science at different levels from the age of 3+ to 17+ itself is a unique experience. The overall objectives of learning experiences are decided ultimately by several factors and mainly by:

1. science teacher,
2. quality of textbook,
3. available teaching aids,
4. general curriculum, and
5. science curriculum.

Every aspect of these five factors contribute to the success or failure of proper science teaching-learning process. The functional objectives in the hierarchical order are:

1. knowledge,
2. understanding,
3. application, and
4. skill.

There is no doubt about the fact that all these four objectives are realised even at the lowest primary level. A child of 3+ or 4+ is curious enough to know the environments and their behaviour. In a play-way method, the child gains knowledge and ends up in showing the skill. The 'Heuristic method' (To discover) is inherent in the child. It needs to be developed.

The learning of Science begins with the principle of child-centredness according to the needs of the pupils at that age. The knowledge, information gradually develop in higher classes wherein the different principles *viz*.:

1. Community-Centredness; (needs of society),
2. Conservation (cherishing the tradition and culture),
3. Activity Centredness (Lab. Activities and field experience),
4. Creativity (creative approach) are given importance.

The children at the primary level are influenced mostly by the environment-physical, social and biological. Thus science at these levels must be taught with emphasis on cleanliness, healthy habits, personal hygiene, sanitation, gardening, and study in general way about certain natural phenomena like weather, universe, planets etc.

At the upper primary level, emphasis should be given on acquisition of knowledge, ability to think logically, drawing conclusions and making decisions. Science should now be taught as Physics, Chemistry, Biology, Astrology etc., in an integrated form as "General Science". There need not necessarily be separate textbooks but one comprehensive textbook with topics in a correlated manner developing with each branch should suffice.

At the senior secondary level (Class XI and XII), Science becomes optional. Some go for arts/commerce stream. The science stream must be for highly talented students with excellent innovative and thinking ability. Here again they can be given the choice of teaching physical science with mathematics as a combination or can combine with natural science (Biology). The in-depth study of each branch begins at XI level.

Integrated Science in Action

We have been advocating integrated approach to science teaching over a decade. Some efforts have been made in this direction but without much success. In some cases, we have decompartmentalised Physics, Chemistry and Biology in a physical manner and put the different branches of science in one textbook labelling it as an "Integrated Science". Integrated Science is more than combining of different branches of science in the same textbook. It is an approach of spontaneous correlation among different disciplines of science. This correlation is natural and needs teachers to be oriented with this approach. This Integrated Science in action has been discussed in detail (with concrete examples) in the next chapter.

References

1 *Source*: Strategies for Developing an Environmental Education Curriculum, Paris, Unesco (1980) and NCERT's approach paper on Environmental Education, 1981.

2 Brunson and Dowling. Suggestions for the teaching of Science in Twelve Year Programme (South Carolina : Department of Education Publication), 1960, p.47.

VI

Development of Exemplar Science Teaching Learning Materials

> There are geniuses in every village, town and city. We must penetrate among the masses, learn from them, organise their experiences into systematic principles and urge them to practice them in order that they may solve their own problems and enjoy freedom and faculty.
> —*Mao Tsetung*

In the earlier chapters some theoretical aspects concerning recent approaches to science teaching have been discussed. These approaches tend to de-emphasise straight memorisation and emphasise understanding in the context of real problems. The most important contribution of the teacher must always be his ability to make interpretations, innovations, invent his own study units and make them come to life by adapting to opportunities in his classroom and- living environment. He must be inventive in demonstrating examples of an idea from the resources at hand in specific situations.

To operationalise recent approaches to science teaching at the elementary level, it may be imperative to elucidate the above recent trends concerning teaching learning science in actual science class teaching. For the convenience of the teacher, some units are discussed keeping in view the syllabus of Science Education at the Primary level (EVS I & II) and Upper Primary level developed on the basis of Ten Year School Curriculum Framework.

The units are as follows:

1. Village Pond—An integrated approach in Environmental Studies at the Primary level.
2. Our Scientific World (Upper Primary level).
3. Heat and Energy charge (Upper Primary level).

4. Chemistry in Home and in Farming (Upper Primary level).
5. Maintaining Good health (Upper Primary level).

These units are arranged into series of activities and a class assessment. The different parts of each activity can be grouped or planned as individual lessons. The class assessment can be used for evaluation of the group to determine whether the behavioural objectives have been satisfied.

The Process

These units are organised to emphasise the processes of learning *i.e.*, observing, informing, classifying, measuring, and communicating. This group of learning skills gives pupils the tools to understand the nature of environment: they help the pupil become involved actively in defining and solving problems.

The process is not taught as an independent area of study, but rather as natural outcomes of an activity oriented programme of specific concepts and content.

The Method

Several of the activities stress the "open handedness" approach without being encumbered with pre-established solutions and "correct" answers.

Pupils learn by doing. The importance of the field trip cannot be overemphasised. Direct experience of observing on a walking trip in the neighbourhood produces learning values that obviously cannot be found in reading books.

When children are involved directly with materials for real purposes, and when the pupils are given substantial motivation and orientation, the teacher's role changes from a dominant leader to that of a guide, observer and participant.

A Final Word

These units are intended to provide an organised group of activities, concepts and objectives. It would be recognised, however, that the teacher can change, delete and add where the teaching and learning in the teacher's judgement could be enhanced. Flexibility in planning and implementing with reference to the varied physical conditions of the school and local community, the wide range of children's ability, and the diversity of experiences which both teachers and pupils bring are important to the school programme.

An Enquiry Approach or Discovery Approach is commonly used in these units.

Environmental Studies Units

In this chapter, the first unit "Village pond" is presented as an example of how an integrated approach is implemented. The remaining three units are meant for imparting environment science education meaningfully. The teacher may use an integrated approach in these three units by the following "Village pond" unit.

Village Pond

Background for the Teacher

All living beings, including man, must have water in order to survive. Although water is in plenty in many areas of the world, it is becoming polluted in intensity. Wasting of water is totally undesirable. Even if water may be available in plenty for our children, they should be sensitised about conservation of water. Children should learn that water is polluted by human waste. As these wastes are dumped in nearby ponds, lakes, streams and rivers, the water from these sources become unfit for human consumption.

In order to have an integrated approach in this unit on "Village Pond", a teacher may introduce this unit with the help of folk-lores that our grand parents tell (near the pond etc.) to the children in the evening. These folk-lores may be suitably used while teaching social studies and languages.

Concepts to be developed

1. Water moves in a cycle from rivers, streams, lakes and other water bodies to become part of the air and clouds and comes back to the earth.
2. Water is necessary for survival
3. There are many kinds of impurities in water
4. Water can be cleaned and used again.

Village Pond

Content	Examples, Material	Activities	Evaluation
Problem I-1			
What is the location of your village pond? Where is your village pond located?	(Geography)	Discuss location of the village with the concept of direction (East, West, North, South).	Answer the following questions. Discuss location of your house with the concept of direction with reference to your school.
Problem I-2			
What are the measurements of the village pond?	Measuring tape in inches and Centimetres) (Mathematics)	Measure the following item of your village pond *i.e.*, length, breadth, area, and depth.	Answer the following questions. Suppose the length of your village pond is 45 ft. and breadth is 20 ft. What will be the area of your pond?
How old is the village pond?			
Problem I-3			
What type of fairs (*melas*) take place near your village pond?		Teacher should discuss the age of the pond; explain the significance of these *melas* with special reference historical implication, if any.	
What are the advantages of village fairs?		Discuss advantages of these *melas* meeting of old friends, exchange of ideas and fun filled activities.	

Contd.

Content	Examples, Material	Activities	Evaluation
Problem I-4			
What are the utilities of the village pond?		Discuss advantages of the village pond with special reference to agricultural aspects, protection of public property, and flowing of rain water in the pond etc.	Write a note on the advantages of a village pond in your notebook.
Problem I-5			
How do we abuse a village pond?	(Civic aspect)	Round table conference. Discuss how we pollute the pond with our human waste. Discuss method of disposal of human waste in the village (*i.e.*, digging ditches and dumping the human waste in these ditches and covering with lye).	
How do we get water in the village pond?		Discuss the source of water in the village pond.	
		Student Activity I	
What are the common sources of water?		Discuss the sources and abundance of water on the earth's surface.	
		Discuss the natural formation of rain water with phenomenon of evaporation and condensation.	

Contd.

Content	Examples, Material	Activities	Evaluation
	Wide, mouthed bottles	*Experiment I-1*	
	Marking pencil, or masking tape or rubber band.	Introduction to Evaporation and condensation	
		Part I Procedure	
		1. Obtain several wide mouthed bottles. Fill the bottles with varying amount of water. Mark the level of the water in bottles with marking tape or rubber bands.	
		2. Place the bottles near window and let them stand.	
		3. After several hours, observe what has happened to the level of water in the bottles. Record these observations in your laboratory note book.	
		4. Leave the bottles untouched near the window overnight.	
		5. Next day observe what has happened to the water level in the jar. Record these observations in your Lab. Note book.	

Contd.

Content	*Examples, Material*	*Activities*	*Evaluation*
		Part II	
		1. Obtain a 500 ml. Beaker. Fill it with 400 ml tap water and add several ice cubes to the water.	
		2. Using a suitable colour (preferably dark) colour the water in the beaker.	Answer the following questions.
		3. After a few minutes, feel the outside of the beaker. Note the colour of the water on the outside of the beaker.	From your observations, attempt to explain from where the water on the outside of the beaker (in Part III) came. Make reference to: "condensation" and "water vapour". Record observations in your books and discuss in class.
Problem I-6			
Is our drinking water in the village fit for consumption?	Example: Apparatus and Material, Village drinking water, Beaker, Wire gauze, spirit lamp, Microscope.	(a) Evaporate some drinkable water in a beaker and discuss your results.	
		(b) Observe sample of drinking water under microscope. Discuss your results in the class room. Discuss the most common impurities in your drinking water.	

Contd.

Content	Examples, Material	Activities	Evaluation
Additional Question			
	Attempt to explain in terms of evaporation and condensation what becomes of water in our oceans, rivers, lakes and atmosphere. Try to devise a cycle to explain the processes involved in the following diagram.	Field Trip I-1	
What are the harmful effects of impure drinking water?	Arrange a field trip to visit the village and observe the impurities in the natural water stored in a pond. The teacher should discuss the danger of typhoid from impure drinking water, and parasites such as amoeba which are serious dangers in impure water.		

Diagramatic Presentation of Water Cycle

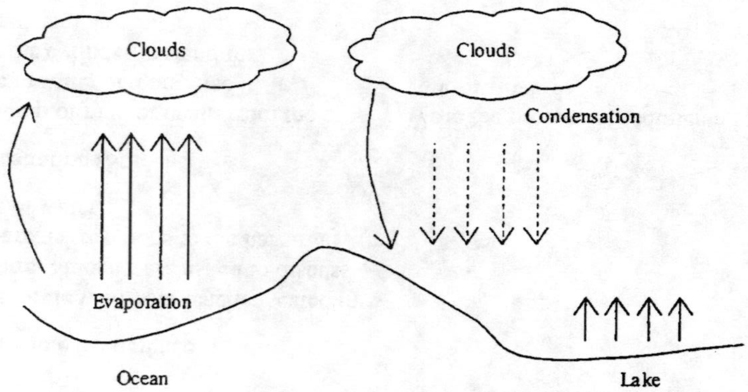

Contd.

Content	*Examples, Material*	*Activities*	*Evaluation*
	Students are asked to discuss at home the harmful effects of impure drinking water. Report the results of discussion in class.	Students will be evaluated with the help of verbal reports of parents.	
		Round Table Conference	
		Sit in a circle with your teacher seated in the centre. Students are asked to discuss their parents' reactions to the harmful effects of water.	
Problem I-F		Demonstration (Student)	
How can we purify our drinking water?	(i) Chalk (ii) Mud (iii) Beaker containing water.	Put a lump of mud or chalk from the village in water and disperse it. Allow the cylinder to stand for 15 minutes.	Write the process of sedimentation in your own words.
		Discuss the use of setting basins in purification of water.	
Sedimentation Filtration	Chalk Gravel, Coarse or fine sand.	Demonstration (Student) Demonstrate the filtration of chalk suspension through a filter-bed consisting of gravel, coarse and fine sand.	

Contd.

Content	*Examples, Material*	*Activities*	*Evaluation*
Aeration	Beaker, Spirit Lamp, Village drinking water.	Taste the village drinking water before boiling and after boiling (a) Spraying water into air (b) Allowing water to flow over rocky masses.	Write the process of filtration in your note book.
Distillation		The teacher should explain the distillation process by reviewing the above process used by village doctor. Tell the student that distillation is one of the most commonly used method for purification in laboratory which the students, have seen in the village doctor's shop (Ayurvedic doctor) Demonstration (Teacher) Set up the distillation equipment. Have the students distilled drinkable water and keep the residue as well as distillate. Have the students discuss the applicability of distillation in the village for purification of drinking water. The teacher should help in concluding the discussion that distillation is a good laboratory method but it is used at a small scale.	

Content	*Examples, Material*	*Activities*	*Evaluation*
Use of bleach (Chlorine is used to kill disease producing bacteria)	Drinking water, Beaker (Bleach)	Experiment (Student) Purify water by the use of bleach. Add a few drops of bleach to the village drinking water.	
		Arrange a trip to visit the nearest town to demonstrate the process of chlorination and filtration used in the Municipal Water Purification Unit.	Write a report on the methods used in the purification of drinking water in your community.
What should be the characteristics of drinking water?	Sample of village drinking water (H^1)	Identify these two samples according to the following table.	Answer the following questions. What causes some water to be different from others?

Data Table

	Water H^1 (Village)	Water H^2 (Pure Water)
Taste		
Colour		
Odour		
Any other difference		
Compare the results with other members of the class.		

Assessment and Evaluation

1. Which picture shows that water can be dangerous to drink?

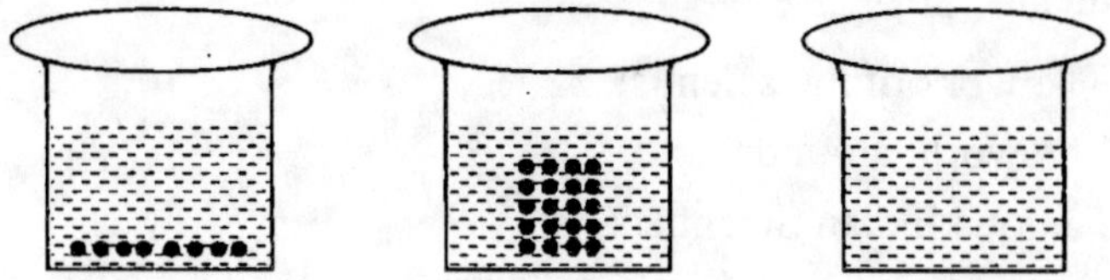

2. Is the drinking water in your community fit for drinking?
3. If your answer to the above question is 'no', make a list of things you could do in your community to improve the quality of drinking water.
4. How can we change drinking water habits of our villagers?
5. How can we purify water at our homes if the chemicals mentioned in this unit are not available?

A final word about general evaluation of a science unit—the following are core criteria which may be used in evaluating a student.

		E G S U
1.	General understanding of the concepts	
2.	Ability to express ideas clearly	
3.	Active participation in the class discussion	
4.	Application of knowledge to the daily life	
5.	Original approach	
6.	Home assignment	
7.	Written exams	
8.	Behaviour change in the pupils	
9.	Observation power	
10.	Forming hypotheses	
11.	Drawing inferences	

*E = Excellent;

G = Good;

S = Satisfactory;

U = Unsatisfactory.

Exemplary Unit

Our Scientific World

Content

A. The work of the scientist

B. The world around us

C. Famous Indian Scientists

Statement of General Objectives

1. The student should demonstrate that he understands the work of the scientist.
2. The student should demonstrate that he understands how the work of the scientist affects him, his family and the community.
3. The student should demonstrate that he understands scientific method and demonstration specific skills such as (i) observation (ii) manipulation, and (iii) classification.
4. The student should demonstrate that he is familiar with his Indian Heritage in the area of science.

Specific Objectives

The student should demonstrate that he understands the work of the scientist (refer to general objectives 1 and 2).

1. In understanding plant kingdom (refer to general objectives 1 and 2)
2. In industry (refer to general objectives 1 and 2)
3. In the area of consumer goods (refer to general objective 2)
4. In protecting the environment (refer to general objective 2)
5. In agriculture (refer to general objective 2)
6. In extending the range of human knowledge (refer to general objective 2)
7. In protecting human and animal life (refer to general objective 2)
8. In the analysis of substances (refer to general objective 1).

General Suggestions to the Teacher in Implementing Objective 1

The successful teaching of this course designed for students in India primarily depends on the abilities, creativity and enthusiasm of the science teacher. Good materials can contribute to making a good course, but the most important source is still the teacher and his alertness in recognising how he can use materials at hand and create and develop others. The purpose of the teaching suggestions is not to lay down hard and fast rules for achievement of the above objectives but to act as a guide. Thus, the science teacher should feel free to use any material which is not listed in this unit in order to help the student understand the work of the scientist. However, the following suggestions should be helpful to the science teacher in order to accomplish the above objective.

1. The teacher should apply the "discovery approach" in dealing with the work of scientists. Rather than giving a lecture, it is more effective for the teacher to arrange a round table conference at which students discuss the role of scientists in developing home products.
2. Field trips to the village should be arranged in order to look for examples of contributions of scientists in the community.
3. If possible, the teacher should obtain the help of educated community members in the community who have been in big cities in leading a discussion about the work of scientists in other walks of life.

   The guest might bring new articles (shave lotion, deodorant, insect repellent and perfumes) to which the students have never been exposed, to make his discussion more meaningful to the students.
4. The answer to any question should not be made readily available to the students. The students should be encouraged to think and struggle with the question. If the question is very difficult, the teacher should help students to find the solution.
5. The list of companies and institutions which distribute on request free useful materials for science teaching may be sought and the teacher should make wide use of this as of any materials his ingenuity can concoct.

Activities, Materials, and Evaluation for Achievement of Unit I (Objective I)

Content	*Examples, Apparatus and Material*	*Activities*	*Evaluation*
Problem I-A:		*Activity No. 1*	
What is the work of the scientist?	Cereals such as wheat, corn, rich barley Legumes such as peas, beans, lentils and peanuts, Sugar, Fertilisers, Grains, Tea from the leaves of the tea plant. Tobacco from the leaves of the nicotine plant, Clothes, Wood.	Set out on a table all the equipment mentioned in the previous column and discuss the uses of plants in our rural life. Emphasise that plants are good factories of our village life. They have been feeding us from generation to generation.	
	Coal, Paper, Rubber, Lumber, Resins.	Every form of animal life is dependent upon plant life. The teacher should point out that it is within the past century that scientists have discovered what takes place in the cells of plants.	Have the students make a collection of press clippings describing plant uses and plant reports.
	Vegetable oils like cotton seed oil, olive oil, palm oil. Dyes of many colours.	During the manufacture of food, and even now, the solution of this problem is far from complete. Generally people do not give much consideration to the significance of plants and plant products.	

Contd.

Content	Examples, Apparatus and Material	Activities	Evaluation
		But the scientists and conservationists have made endless efforts to change man's attitude towards plants. As a result of the detailed studies by scientists of plants, their structure and their various functions. The average man is beginning to appreciate the importance of plants. The scientists have helped the average man through their studies to produce healthier plants, discover new uses of various plants, thus improving the life in general and making us more aware of our dependence upon plants for goods, fuel and industrial products.	Have the student write a report on the uses of plants to man. Using an outline; map of India have the students show the distribution of more important plants in different states of our country.
		Activity No. II	
	The following are some of the suggested local resources in the community (a) Agriculture Inspector (b) Block Development Officer (B.D.O.) (c) Hospital Doctor	Have the students investigate by inquiry at home from local resources, some articles made by chemists of present day use, unknown thirty years ago.	

Contd.

Content	*Examples, Apparatus and Material*	*Activities*	*Evaluation*
	(d) Educated persons of the community who have visited or stayed in big cities.		
		Activity No. III	
	Some students may bring the fact that about thirty years ago malaria used to be considered a fatal disease.	The teacher may have a round table conference and lead a discussion about the information obtained by the students from Activity No. II. The teacher should discuss that many animals (cows, buffaloes, horses) become victims of diseases which were then incurable resulting in the death of the animals. This was a great financial setback for a poor farmer, but most of the common diseases of animals which were once fatal can now be cured easily by modern medicines. These medicines are often chemical compounds synthesised by chemists.	The students will be evaluated corresponding to their participation in the round table conference.
	Veterinary Doctor	If possible, a lecture from a veterinary doctor would be quite informative. The teacher should also discuss the contributions of science in textiles, vitamins, nutrients and insecticides.	

Contd.

Content	Examples, Apparatus and Material	Activities	Evaluation
		Activity No. IV	
	Nylon, Plastic Dyes, D.D.T. Fertilisers.	Have the students study articles and products (e.g., nylon, plastic dyes, DDT etc.) made by scientists and discuss the work of scientists in the making of these products.	The students will be evaluated from their active participation in the class.
		Activity No. V	
	The teacher should arrange a trip to nearby industry. For example; — Firestone Tire Factory, —Bata Shoe Company and Escorts Tractor Company etc.	Field Trip No.1 Arrange a field trip to a factory near the village and discuss the work of the scientist.	
		Activity No. VI	
		The teacher should arrange a visit to the local dispensary and elucidate the work of the scientists. A member of local health unit may be requested to speak on insecticides and chemicals used in water purification and sewage disposal.	
		Pharmacist (Compounded in Indian terms) can elaborate the work of the chemist by giving	The students will be evaluated according to

Contd.

Content	*Examples, Apparatus and Material*	*Activities*	*Evaluation*
		some examples of modern medicine. After the .visit to the local dispensary, the teacher should discuss the role of scientists.in modern medicines	their participation in the discussion.
		Activity No. VII	
		The teacher can request some of the major petroleum companies (e.g., Indian Oil Company to show a film on the exploration and refining of crude oil emphasising the work of the scientists. If the film cannot be arranged, the teacher can write to these organisations for pictures illustrating the refining of petroleum and the work of the scientists.	The students are asked to write a short report on the film, emphasising the work of the scientist in the refining of petroleum.
		After showing the film, the teacher should have a round table conference and discuss the role of the scientist in the petroleum industry.	The students will be evaluated from their participation in the round table conference.
		Demonstration	
	Distillation Flask, Spirit Lamp, Stand, Crude oil (Bunsen Burner if it is available)	The teacher should carry out distillation of crude oil which can be easily obtained from a bullock cart owner.	The students are required to record the observation in their

Contd.

Content	Examples, Apparatus and Material	Activities	Evaluation
			laboratory notebooks and discuss the above observations in the class.
		Activity No. VIII Have the students discuss each film and visit (refer to Activity IV, V and VI) explaining the work of the scientist in each of the above activities, thus reviewing the work of the scientists in industry.	The students are asked to submit a report on each film, emphasising the work of the scientists. The student should be able to list facts and concepts learned.
		Activity No. IX *Demonstration I:* Preparation of Soap. Soap is made by boiling together either sodium or potassium hydroxide and some vegetable oil or animal fat (olive oil, palm oil, or cotton seed oil). Alkali + fat $\rightarrow$ Soap + glycerine.	

Contd.

Content	*Examples, Apparatus and Material*	*Activities*	*Evaluation*
		Lab Instructions	
	80 grams of cotton seed, oil, Beaker (100 ml) Water, Thermometer Stirring rod, Spirit lamp.	Melt about 80 grams of cotton seed oil. Dissolve 20 grams of lye in 40 ml of water. Pour the hot oil into the lye solution a little at a time stirring constantly and keeping the temperature below the boiling point. Heat for half an hour, then cool. Remove the cake of soap and test its action in water.	
		Demonstration II:	
		Preparation of toothpaste and powder.	
	Table salt, Baking soda, Beaker	Method I – An inexpensive but effective toothpowder can be prepared by mixing one part (by weight) of powdered table salt and two parts of baking soda.	The students will be evaluated from the following question verbally. What ingredient is used in toothpaste for the purpose of (a) Neutralising mouth acids? (b) Avoiding decay dental carries?

Contd.

Content	*Examples, Apparatus and Material*	*Activities*	*Evaluation*
		The salt serves as an astringent and the bicarbonate reacts with food particles in the mouth.	
		Activity No. X	
The scientist is important in manufacturing consumer goods.		It is quite feasible to have a film show regarding manufacture of consumer goods by requesting some of the major firms. For example, Hindustan Lever.	The students are asked to submit a short report giving the major ingredients and
		(Lifeboy and Sunlight Soap) has moving vans showing the films about their products in daily use for publicity.	methods of preparation of the following consumer goods.
		The above activities demonstrate the work of the scientists in the area of consumer goods: (a) soap (b) toothpaste	
		Activity No. XI	
		Demonstration III:	
The scientists help us keep healthy	Drinking water, Beaker, Wire gauze, Spirit lamp	Evaporate some drinking water in a beaker and show the residue to the students. The students are led into discussion and some information may be given that natural water contains dissolved gases, mineral salts and bacteria.	

Contd.

Content	*Examples, Apparatus and Material*	*Activities*	*Evaluation*
		Activity No. XII	
		Arrange a trip to a village doctor practising Indian medicine. Ask the students to observe the distillation of some of Indian medicines. Tell the students that there are various methods of purification of water. One of the most common methods used in the laboratory.	The students are asked to submit a report on the following project and discuss it in the class: "How the scientists can help us in
		is distillation. Mention some of the methods used in making water potable. For example; sedimentation, coagulation, filtration, aeration. Tell the students that these methods will be discussed in detail in Unit III.	protection of our environment?"
Scientists help us dispose human waste.		Have the students explain the effective methods of disposal of human waste by digging ditches and dumping the human waste in the ditches and covering with lye, which is a chemical compound. This would reduce the number of flies which are the source of many diseases. The teacher should discuss air pollution around the village and the world by showing some pictures illustrating the problem of air pollution and how we can overcome it by scientific methods.	The students will be evaluated according to their participation in the class.

Contd.

Content	Examples, Apparatus and Material	Activities	Evaluation
		Demonstration	
	Carbon, Sulphur, Spirit lamp/ Bunsen Burner	The teacher should demonstrate the problem of air pollution by the actual burning of sulphur and carbon resulting in the formation of SO_2 and CO_2. The above activities demonstrate the work of the scientists in protecting the environment.	The students are asked to submit a report on the problem of air pollution in the village.
		Activity No. XIII	
Scientist help make the soil more productive.	Agriculture Inspector	Invite an agriculture inspector to give a lecture on the scientific farming which requires knowledge of the chemistry of soils and fertilisers. The teacher should elaborate the contribution of the scientists in the manufacture of fertilisers.	
		Activity No. XIV	
	Two plants, Fertiliser	Have the students grow two plants under similar conditions; one with fertiliser and the other without fertiliser. Ask the students to submit a short report explaining the difference in the rate of growth of these plants. Tell the students the role of science in extending the range of human knowledge. Science has entered our daily life,	The students will be evaluated from their reports explaining the role of fertiliser in growth of plants. The students are asked to make a collection of

Contd.

Content	Examples, Apparatus and Material	Activities	Evaluation
		that reference to science matters in newspapers and magazines and in conversation are common. The teacher should also emphasise cultural values of science. A well educated person is one who has a general acquaintance with many fields of knowledge. The student should be able to understand what is written in scientific books, magazines and newspapers.	clippings from daily newspapers which deal with scientific research, industries or new products. Students will be evaluated according to the number of clippings which deal with science.
		Activity No. XV	
Scientists improve the quality of human and animal life.		The teacher may request some pharmaceutical firms, e.g., Merck Sharp and Dohme and Ranbaxy, for a film show concerning the manufacture of drugs and their use in the protection of human and animal life. After the film show, the teacher should arrange a round table conference and discuss the benefits of medicines in human and animal life.	The students are asked to write a report on the benefits of medicine in human and animal life.
		Activity No. XVI	
Scientist analyse the substances.	Mercuric Oxide Spirit lamp/Bunsen Burner Test tube	Heat Mercuric Oxide to illustrate analysis. Have the students state observations after the demonstration. The teacher should state the methods by which a chemist determines the composition of matter.	

Contd.

Content	*Examples, Apparatus and Material*	*Activities*	*Evaluation*
		Activity No. XVII	
	Beaker, Water, Sulphuric acid Electrodes Batteries or electric supply	Pass an electric current through acidified water to illustrate chemical composition of water. Test the presence of hydrogen and oxygen by glowing splinter.	The students are required to write observations in their notebooks and discuss their observations in the class.
		Activity No. XVIII	
	Zinc Hydrochloric Acid	Mix Zinc and Hydrochloric Acid in a test tube. Test the presence of Hydrogen by glowing splinter and evaporate Zinc Chloride solution.	

Evaluation of Objective 1

In order to evaluate the first objective, as a whole, the teacher should evaluate each of the activities as suggested and grade the student according to the extent of his comprehension and appreciation of the work of the scientist.

The following is a word of caution in assessing these criteria. The teacher should make sure that the student has not merely memorised facts but also understands the work of the scientists. Three simple methods of determining the students' ability are mentioned below:

1. Class participation in discussions and field trips, variety and quality of students' questions and their sincere efforts to find solutions to the problems.
2. Written reports on various aspects such as air and water pollution in the village.
3. Written quiz.
4. Quality of laboratory work. (Note: field trips and activities VIII, X, XI, XIII, etc., constitute lab. Work).

However, the following two activities might be helpful to the teacher in ascertaining that the students have understood the work of the scientists:

1. Bring some articles of daily use, including some which do not involve chemical process and set them out on a table. Ask the students to eliminate those substances which are not developed by scientific processes.
2. Have one group of students submit a report on industrial science, a second group on consumer science, a third group on environmental science, a fourth group on agricultural science, a fifth group on medical science and a sixth group on extending the nature of human knowledge. Collect the reports, evaluate them and have students give a panel discussion in class.

The purpose of this discussion is to allow students to pursue a field in which they have more interest and present their findings to the class. After the discussion, each student should write a report on all aspects of science emphasising the role of science as it pertains to him.

Table

Content	*Examples, Apparatus and Material*	*Activities*	*Evaluation*
		Activity No. XIX	
Problem I-B What is the world around us made of?		(a) Set out on a table all the equipment mentioned in the previous column and discuss the contribution of science in the making of these substances.	The students prepare a list of the substances available at home involving the applications of science and discuss in class.
	Rock, Paper, Cloth, Water, Fertilisers	(b) Have the students investigate, categorise and describe the applications of science in the surroundings of their own village. Have the student eliminate those substances which are not developed through scientific processes.	
		(c) Have the students discuss Activities No. III and IV suggested earlier in order to help them understand how the work of scientists affects him, his family and the village life.	
		Activity No. XX	
Science is important in our daily life.		*Visit to a village Potter's wheel:* The teacher should arrange a visit to a village potter's wheel. Pottery is generally made by turning a piece of plastic clay on a wheel. All clay products are baked in furnaces called kilns. During heating,	

Contd.

Content	*Examples, Apparatus and Material*	*Activities*	*Evaluation*
		strong crystals form which make up the hard materials of bricks and dishes. Glazed dishes and tiles are made in much the same way, except that a coating of some chemicals, that are the raw materials for a low temperature glass are coated on to the clay and baked. The village potter sometimes uses molten salt for a decorative glaze. The above activity demonstrates the importance of science in village life.	
		Activity No. XXI	
	Tools or machines employed by the farmer in the farm such as spades, rake, crow bars, wedge, shovel, tongs, wheel-barrow. Kitchen aids such as sugar tongs, nut crackers, knives and spoons.	Set out a table all the equipment mentioned in the previous column and discuss that man has invented tools of many types to lighten his work. These labour saving devices mentioned above make the work about home and farm less difficult and more interesting through application of scientific principles in these tools. Tell the students that the above tools will be discussed in detail.	Make a list of all machines, either simple or compound used in or about your home which use some scientific principles.
		Activity No. XXII	
	Soap Cosmetics, Disinfectants Fertilisers	Ask the students to describe what life would be without the following substances: soap, tooth powder, cosmetics,	

Contd.

Content	*Examples, Apparatus and Material*	*Activities*	*Evaluation*
		disinfectants. The teacher should discuss many products of scientific nature which are used in the rural life. Ask students to solve the following problems by using materials that are the result of science technology: (a)to remove spots and stains from clothes (b)to extinguish fire (c) to cure diseases like malaria, typhoid, flu	
Science helps in understand-ing our bodies.		The teacher should tell the students that eating is not only one of the most enjoyable activities, but also one of most essential activities for the body's development. The teacher should also explain the importance of a proper and balanced diet in the human body. Provide a sample of a balanced diet. The teacher should also discuss the harmful effects of undesirable and rotten food.	The students will be evaluated from their active participation in the discussion and in a report about the balanced diet.
Food can be saved from spoiling by using vinegar as a preservative		Have the students discuss and make a report about the balanced diet which an average person should take. Tell the students that the above activities on balanced diet would be discussed in detail at later stage.	
	Pictures of rats or person showing unbalanced diet.	The teacher should exhibit the pictures of rats or persons eating unbalanced and poor diets, *e.g.*, knock knees, bow-legs, anaemia.	

Objective 2

The Student should understand how the work of the scientist affects him, his family and the village.

General Suggestions to the Teacher in Implementing Objective 2.

1. The teacher should correlate content with the character of daily life. For example, discuss how an understanding of science will make a person a better farmer, a better nurse or a better citizen. The teacher should discuss the value of science in all walks of life.
2. The teacher should use the investigation approach and encourage the students to participate in the discussion on applications of science in the village life.
3. The teacher should not ridicule any question. Some questions may be irrelevant. These should be directed in a constructive discussion.

Evaluation of Objective 2

In order to secure a reliable evaluation of the accomplishments of a pupil in this objective, it is necessary to make assessments of the component parts of a unit, such as the individual problems in this objective, as mentioned earlier. The teacher should utilise all evaluation techniques mentioned earlier. For example, the teacher should grade students according to the following criteria:

1. Participation in class discussion
2. Reports
3. Written quiz, a subjective type or an objective type of question may be used (refer to the same question given below).

In addition to the above evaluation procedures, a subjective type of question may be used as the supplementary portion of an objective question. The following example would elucidate the above conviction.

Subjective Type of Question	*Objective Type of Question*
Write a short essay on the contributions of scientists in the improvement of daily life.	Please use + for true and 0 for false. Science has specific application in the following aspects of our life activities. (a) Reducing human sufferings (b) Consumer goods (c) Cleanliness (hygienic living)

Furthermore, the teacher should give subjective types of questions in the form of problems where students learn to think.

Objective 3

The student should demonstrate that he understands scientific method and demonstrate specific skills such as (i) observation, (ii) manipulation, and (iii) classification.

Suggestions of Teacher in Implementing Objective 3

1. The scientist employs an orderly method of thinking known as scientific method. In the opinion of this writer, scientific method as a rote item in the curriculum has little value; its value should be realised by actually applying it in teaching. The teacher should actually use the scientific method in experiments, demonstrations and classroom work and tell the students when scientific method is being used, giving instances where scientists used scientific methods in preparing new substances or seeking answers to problems.
2. The teacher should show all the equipment kept in the lab and explain the function of each item.
3. The teacher should advise the students to make clear and accurate records at the time of observations of what they have observed. The experiments should not be done in a mechanical manner. The students should be sent to the lab to investigate various scientific principles. Too much time should not be spent on getting the correct results which gives a false concept of the whole scientific endeavour.

Laboratory Activities XXVIII

Contents	*Examples, Apparatus and Material*	*Activities*	*Evaluation*
		Experiment No. I *(Observation and Laboratory Method)* *Exercise I-A*	
	In general, the following observations should be made. Science equipment present in the laboratory. Number of doors, windows and desks	How well do you observe? Have the students look around the classroom and laboratory. "List four observations that you think are most significant. Compare your observations with those made by other students in your class."	The students are required to record the observations in their laboratory notebooks and discuss the observations in the class.
		Exercise I-B	
	Candle Ruler (for measurement of length, height and diameter of the candle) Tin lid, Match box	"What observations can be made on a burning candle?" The teacher should help the students in making observations and inference in the above experiment.	Same as above.
		Exercise I-C	
		"What is the common laboratory equipment?" The students should prepare a	The students will be evaluated from the list of equipment and

Contd.

Contents	*Examples, Apparatus and Material*	*Activities*	*Evaluation*
		list of the common laboratory equipment present in the laboratory and discuss the use of each piece of equipment.	also from their participation in the class.
		Exercise I-D	
		"What thing you must do in cleaning up your place at the end of the laboratory?"	The students will be evaluated by the teacher's inspection at their stations.
		Exercise I-E	
	Test tube, Spirit lamp/Bunsen Burner.	"What precautions must be taken while heating a test tube?"	The students will be evaluated while doing actual experimentation.
	Ice, Beaker, Spirit Lamp/Bunsen Burner.		
Problem I-C		*Exercise I-F*	
What is a physical change? Any change in matter which		*Demonstration:* Melt ice and boil water to form steam. The teacher should tell the students that	The students will be asked to write in their notebooks three examples of physical
does not destroy the identity of a		in the above example mater has undergone change. Its form may not be the same, but	changes related to their home life.

Contd.

Contents	*Examples, Apparatus and Material*	*Activities*	*Evaluation*
substance or change its characteristic properties is a physical change. It is a temporary change.		the matter has not lost its identity. Such a change is called physical change.	
Problem I-D		*Exercise I-G*	
What is a chemical change?	Wood, Spirit lamp, Test tube, Zinc Hydrochloric Acid	*Demonstration:* Ask the students to observe a change in the following demonstration and write it in their notebooks: (a) burn wood (b) react zinc with diluted Hydro Chloric Acid in a test tube.	The student will be evaluated from their participation in the above demonstration.
In a chemical change, new substance with new properties is formed.		Have the students tell the difference between this change and the above change. The teacher should tell very clearly that in each of these changes the identity of the original substance or substances are lost. These are called chemical changes.	The students will be evaluated from the following question: Which of the following are physical changes: (a) The baking of *Roti* (b) The burning of coal (c) The decay of food (d) The rusting of a shovel (e) The burning of a candle

Contd.

Contents	Examples, Apparatus and Material	Activities	Evaluation
Problem I-E		*Activity No. XXIV*	
Who are the famous Indian scientists?	Pictures of well known scientists of India	The teacher should describe the achievements of Indian scientists (a) C.V. Raman (b) Sir J.C. Bose (c) H. Khorana (d) Aryabhata	Have the students prepare a short written report on one of the scientists not listed?
		Activity No. XXV	
	Biographies of: C.V. Raman Sir J.C. Bose Ramanujan Chander Shekhar Aryabhatta (6th Century, A.D) Bhaskara (12th Century)	Have the students read the biographies of the most eminent scientists of India mentioned in adjacent column?	Have the students write a report on the life of an Indian scientist of whom they like most and why?

4. The teacher can make use of an ordinary note book as a laboratory note book as most of the students especially in the village may not be able to afford purchase of a standard laboratory note book. Keeping a permanent and neat record of observations is a part of scientific training. In the opinion of this writer, the students should hand in a carbon copy of their laboratory work at the end of the period. The carbon copies should be marked and returned to the students to be filed with completed reports.
5. In India, especially in rural high schools, there is an acute shortage of proper lab equipment. A resourceful teacher can overcome this problem to a certain extent by constructing various models in order to illustrate various scientific principles. For example, the teacher can make the model of a fire extinguisher.

Evaluation of Objective 3

1. To evaluate the students' familiarity with the tools of the scientists, an assessment should be made on the performance of the student in actual experimentation during laboratory activities.
2. As mentioned earlier, scientific methods as a rote item in the curriculum has little value. Thus, difficulty of evaluating the comprehension of scientific method by the student is inherent. In the opinion of this writer, the value and training's obtained from the scientific method should be transferable into the students regular walks of life. For example, students should be able to tackle any problem in their lives in a scientific manner which consists of the following four steps:
    1. Making an accurate survey of the problem,
    2. Setting up the method of attacking the problem,
    3. Collecting data regarding problem,
    4. Drawing conclusions from the data which have been collected.

    Scientific method should be evaluated from two points of view:

    1. In terms of what one does
    2. In terms of one's attitude or way of thinking. Both must be taken together to get the true picture of the understanding of scientific method.

In planning learning experiences for developing of skills of problem solving, the teacher should keep in mind that pupils learn to think.

The following problem should be helpful in evaluating the understanding of scientific method.

Problem—"Name some things that you want science to take care of in the community."

Then set up a possible solution to these. Thus, the students should be evaluated from their performance in solving the problem.

Objective 4

The student should become familiar with his Indian heritage in the area of science.

Suggestions to the Teacher in Implementing Objective 4

1. In the opinion of this writer, the most important thing a science teacher can do is to develop the students pride in their scientific culture. It is necessary for a science teacher to believe basically in the competence of Indian scientists.
2. The teacher should present the achievement of Indian scientists to arouse a sense of pride in their accomplishments in the field of science.
3. Inform the students that inspite of lack of financial resources, our country, BHARAT (India), has made major contributions in the scientific world.
4. Biographies of various scientists are readily available in various libraries.
5. Tell the students that every person cannot be a Noble Prize winner like C.V. Raman, but still everyone can contribute something worthwhile to the scientific world according to one's capacity. The most significant contribution to the scientific world in their community is to improve the living conditions of the same. For example, many of us have unhygienic habits of living (impure drinking water, flies causing diseases, and not cleaning our body). We can improve these conditions in our environment and contribute to the scientific world which is concerned with the benefit of mankind.

Heat and Energy Change *(Suggested Time: 3 weeks)*

Content

1. Attributes of a desirable fuel.
2. Fuels used in our homes.
3. Fire extinguisher.
4. Radioactivity, nuclear energy.

Objectives

To familiarise the students with the knowledge of fuels and combustion and their applications in daily life.

Teaching Suggestions

In Indian villages, fuel and combustion are two important aspects. In winter, the villagers use fuels to keep their houses warm as there is no central heating system as in the Western hemisphere. The commonly used fuel is dung cakes. These dung cakes are the best fertilisers which can be used as a manure; but due to lack of scientific knowledge, this manure is being wasted as a cheap fuel.

The teacher should invite an agriculture inspector to explain the uses of dung cakes as a fertiliser.

Chemistry in Home and in Farming
(Suggested Time: 6 Weeks)

Content

1. Chemistry of building material.
2. Chemicals that remove dirt and stains from the Home.
3. To remove spots and stains from clothes.
4. Mineral fertilisers.
5. Pesticide, antiseptic and disinfectant.

Objectives

1. To familiarise the students with the application of chemistry in the home and in farming.
2. To emphasise the importance of chemistry in the students' daily life.

Heat and Energy Change

Contents	Examples, Apparatus and Material	Activities	Evaluation
Problem VII-A	Soft wood, Hard wood, Test tube	Give a lecture on the concept of the calorie by comparing with food calories and the B.T.U. as units of heat measure. Have the students compare soft and hard wood with respect to their use as a fuel and perform destructive distillation.	The students are required to write a short summary on the attributes of a desirable fuel in their own words.
		The teacher can use a coffee can or even a test tube to demonstrate destructive distillation of wood. Have the students discuss the products obtained and their uses.	
		Have the students discuss the attributes of a desirable fuel at home and report their findings at school.	
		The teacher should emphasise that the dung cake is the best manure and is being wasted as a cheap fuel.	
		Have the students discuss the replacement of fuel of dung cakes and emphasise that wood or coal can be used as an effective fuel.	The students are asked to write a report on various fuels which can be used in place of dung cakes.

Contd.

Contents	*Examples, Apparatus and Material*	*Activities*	*Evaluation*
		Guest Speaker (Agriculture Inspector) Arrange a lecture by an Agriculture Inspector to explain the value of dung cakes as a fertiliser in farming. He can also review the other fertilisers, which they have studied earlier. He should also discuss the ways to burn fuels for maximum efficiency.	The students are required to write a report on the value of dung cakes as a fertiliser.
Problem VII-B			
What is a fire extinguisher?	Model of fire extinguisher	Demonstrate the action using a simple model of a fire extinguisher. The teacher should give a lecture on the chemistry involved, the purpose of each part, each substance and how it extinguishes a fire. Have the students construct the model of soda acid fire extinguisher and discuss the places where this type is especially effective, e.g., refer to oil delivery truck in your community.	The students are asked to write a report on fire extinguisher in their own words.
Problem VII-C			
What is Radioactivity?		Give a lecture on the discovery of radium by Madame Curie. Give an elementary idea of disintegration of nucleus. Describe emission of α and β; particles and γ radiations. Have the students discuss the physiological effects of radiation on tissue, cancer.	

Contd.

Contents	*Examples, Apparatus and Material*	*Activities*	*Evaluation*
Problem VII-D			
What are peaceful uses of nuclear energy?		Give a lecture on artificial radioactivity. Have the students discuss peaceful uses of nuclear energy: (a) Use of radioactive isotopes as tracers in research. (b) Use of radio isotopes in industry. (c) Use of nuclear reactors as sources of electric power. (d) Use of nuclear radiation in medicine.	The students are asked to write a report on the peaceful uses of nuclear energy.

Chemistry in Home and in Farming

Contents	*Examples, Apparatus and Material*	*Activities*	*Evaluation*
Problem IV-A			
What is the chemistry of building materials?	Cement, Lime, Plaster, Glass Insulating material	Exhibit the most important chemical materials used in building materials, *e.g.*, cement, lime, plaster, glass, insulating material.	
		The teacher should exhibit some new materials in the class, *e.g.*, insulating material so that while constructing homes, the students might use these material to prevent the loss of heat in the winter.	The students are asked to make a list of the important chemical substances in building material.
		Field Trip Arrange a field trip to study the use of material and effects of weather on those materials in the community.	
Problem IV-B		*Demonstration IV-A*	
What are the chemicals that remove dirt and stains from the homes?	Chlorine Water, Bleach, Beaker	Place a sample of dried unbleached muslin and also a wet sample of the same material in a jar of chlorine gas (If bleach is available, it should be preferred).	The students are required to write the observations in their notebooks and write down the action of bleach on the dirt.

Contd.

Contents	*Examples, Apparatus and Material*	*Activities*	*Evaluation*
		Give a lecture emphasising the chemistry of the bleaching of vegetable fibres by chlorine or bleach.	
		Have the students discuss the process of bleaching as a chemical process of changing the natural colouring matter of textile into colour less compounds.	The students are asked to write an operational definition of the process of bleaching in their own words in their notebooks.
		The teacher should give a lecture on the role of chlorine and oxygen in bleaching.	
		Demonstration IV-B Cleaning with Soap	
(b) Soap	Sodium hydroxide, Vegetable or animal fat or oil Beaker	Prepare a sample of soap by heating animal and vegetable fat or oil, bring to a boil in a solution of sodium hydroxide. When the process is finally judged complete, the mixture of soap glycerol and water is separated by adding salt, the soap rises to the top of kettle. Demonstrate the cleaning of a soiled fabric in water with and without soap. Emphasise that soap is necessary to remove dirt in laundering and it is very important to clean the body with soap as it kills certain bacteria. Also emphasise that cleanliness is very important for our life. Give a lecture on the theory of the action of soap. Explain to the students that the dirt is not attracted to water, does not dissolve or disperse in water.	

Contd.

Contents	*Examples, Apparatus and Material*	*Activities*	*Evaluation*
		In the case of soap, groups of soap ions clump together in ball-like shapes with their hydrocarbon ends towards the centre and the salt end towards water. The water insoluble portions are shielded from the water by the water soluble portions, thus preventing the soap from separating out of solution. At the surface of some oil the hydrophilic portion (carboxyl group) is attracted to the water. With sufficient agitation, the oil can be broken up into tiny droplets. If detergent is available in the community, the teacher should discuss the role of detergent in removing dirt from clothes. Give a lecture on the uses of by-products of glycerine.	The students are asked to summarise steps needed in making of a soap in their notebooks.
		Demonstration IV-C	
		Have the students demonstrate the difference between the following cylinders containing : (a) Water and oil (b) Water, oil and soap	The students will be evaluated from their verbal response on the action of water oil mixture and water, oil and soap mixture.

Contd.

Contents	Examples, Apparatus and Material	Activities	Evaluation
Problem IV-C			
How to remove spots and stains from the clothes?	Clothes with stains Benzene, Methyl Alcohol, Carbon Tetrachloride	Have the students bring the clothes from their homes which have stains of ink, rust, paint, grease. Give a lecture on the usage of organic solvents like Benzene, Methyl Alcohol, Carbon tetrachloride to clean and remove the spots and stains from the clothes.	The students are asked to write a report on health hazards and the use of solvents in their notebooks.
		Mention some of the health hazards of using these solvents, e.g., poisonous vapours, explosive vapours, materials injurious to the skin.	
Problem IV-D			
What are mineral fertilisers?	Common fertilisers which are used in farming	Have the students discuss the role of mineral fertilisers (nitrate, phosphate, potassium and nitro fertilisers) in farming. Their composition and their simple properties and methods of identification should be discussed.	The students are required to write a report on the advantages of fertilisers in farming and the need of proper application.
		Field Trip	
		Arrange a trip to the farms in the community and explain the uses of different types of fertilisers.	

Contd.

Contents	*Examples, Apparatus and Material*	*Activities*	*Evaluation*
	Plant Fertilisers	*Experiment IV-A*	
		Have the students grow the plants with and without fertilisers. The students should take different amounts of fertilisers and a record should be kept for maximum growth of a plant with certain amount of fertiliser.	The students are asked to record their observations in their notebooks and discuss in the class.
Problem IV-E			
What are pesticides, antiseptic and disinfectants?			
(a) Pesticide	Common pesticide D.D.T.	Exhibit some common pesticides and point out that most pesticides are poisonous.	
		Demonstration IV-D	
		Have the students kill insects which are harmful to mankind (mosquitoes) with pesticide.	The students are asked to record their observations in their notebooks and discuss in the class.

Contd.

Contents	*Examples, Apparatus and Material*	*Activities*	*Evaluation*
(b) Antiseptic	Dettol Hydrogen Peroxide Alum	*Demonstration IV-E*	
		Exhibit some common antiseptics and define their uses. The teacher should define antiseptic as chemicals which are used on living tissues to prevent or arrest the growth of harmful organisms.	
(c) Disinfectant		*Demonstration IV-F*	
	Common disinfectants available in the community.	Exhibit some of the common disinfectants to the students and define disinfectants as chemicals which are used on inanimate materials to kill the growth of harmful micro organisms.	The students are asked to describe in writing the difference between pesticide and antiseptic and disinfectant in their notebooks.
Problem IV-F		*Experiment IV-B*	
How to make toothpaste?	Chalk ($CaCO_3$) Magnesia (MgO) Soap or other detergent Alcohol and water	Have the students make tooth powder in the class by mixing the following ingredients : (a) Chalk (b) Magnesia (c) Detergent (d) Flavour (e) Alcohol and water	The students are asked to write the answer for the following questions in their notebooks.

Contd.

Contents	*Examples, Apparatus and Material*	*Activities*	*Evaluation*
		The teacher should explain the uses of these reagents. Ask the students to clean their teeth with their self made tooth paste and take it to their homes and use it. The teacher should also explain the presence of bacteria on uncleaned teeth.	In home made tooth powder, what ingredient is used for the purpose of (a) Scouring and cleaning of teeth? (b) Neutralising mouth acids? (c) Providing a refreshing after taste?
Summary Question			
How are you going to apply the knowledge of chemistry in your daily life?		Have the students discuss this question at home and report the discussion in their notebooks.	
		Round Table Conference	
		The students are asked to discuss the above report in this conference giving their own views and their parents' reactions.	The students will be evaluated from their participation in the conference.

Teaching Suggestions

This is the most important unit in the course content. The teacher should put life in this unit, as it largely depends on him how he arouses the interest of the students in the activities mentioned in this unit. He should try to use local resources, especially parents. The main purpose of this unit is to make the students understand and realise the importance of chemistry in their daily life.

The teacher should arrange field trips with some constructive results. In the opinion of this writer, discussions should be arranged at the farms, as this would bring school activity close to the community. He can supplement the discussion in the field and in the class.

There is no need for having descriptive type of examination. The evaluation should be made by the active participation of students in class discussions.

Maintaining Good Health *(Suggested Time: 5 weeks)*

Content

1. Chemical organisation of the body
2. Food
3. Vitamins
4. Balanced diet
5. Chemotherapy
6. Nature of patent medicines
7. Good living habits

Objectives

1. To familiarise the students with the application of chemistry in the home and in farming.
2. To emphasise importance of chemistry in the students' daily life.

Maintaining Good Health

Contents	*Examples, Apparatus and Material*	*Activities*	*Evaluation*
Problem V-A			
What is the chemical composition of the human body?	Microscope	Give a lecture on composition of the human body emphasising that it is roughly 72 per cent oxygen, 14 per cent carbon, 9 per cent hydrogen, 25 per cent nitrogen and the remaining 3 per cent is composed of other elements like calcium, phosphorus, sodium, chlorine and sulphur.	
		Demonstration V-A	
		Examine any part of the living organism under a microscope. Living organism is made up of little divisions called cells. Give a lecture on the chemical composition of the cells which are filled with a colloidal material or gel containing proteins and water. (These proteins are nitrogenous compounds)	The students are asked to write a report about the composition of human body in their notebooks.
Problem V-B :			
What is food?		Have the students discuss definition of food and aid the students in arriving at a conclusion that food is a chemical substance which provides material for body growth.	
		Give a lecture on essential ingredients of our food. The teacher should explain the fact that the body tissues are	The students are required to write a report on the

Contd.

Contents	*Examples, Apparatus and Material*	*Activities*	*Evaluation*
		largely proteins, their growth and replacement require foods containing similar materials which means that proteins must be contained in some of the foods we eat. Young people should take food rich in proteins, e.g., milk, peas, cheese. Tell the students that carbohydrates are also the sources of energy.	importance of proteins in our food.
Problem V-C			
What are vitamins?	If possible, arrange to have some common vitamins, for example : B.G. Phos. Vitamin A, B and C tablets	Give a lecture on the role of vitamins in our food. Give the definition of vitamins as organic compounds found in certain foods and they have a regulatory action in the human body. Also explain the effect of lack of vitamins in our food. Provide a table which lists the important vitamins and show their relation to health.	The students are required to write a report on which foods in their diets provide which vitamins.
Problem V-D		Have the students review the chemical organisation of the human body and discuss the composition of the human body. Tell the students that the human body cannot create any chemical elements but can only recombine elements supplied in food. Emphasise the fact that in order to assure ourselves of the necessary food materials we should eat what is called a balanced diet. The teacher should exhibit pictures illustrating various diseases (rickets, bone malformation) due to unbalanced diet.	Ask the students to answer the following question: Why should we take a balanced diet?

Contd.

Contents	*Examples, Apparatus and Material*	*Activities*	*Evaluation*
	Standard balanced diet table in terms of calories (It can be obtained from some Government Hospital)	Emphasise the fact that eating is not only one of the most enjoyable activities but is also one of the most essential activities for development of human body. Failure to eat proper and balanced diet is to invite diseases in the human body.	
		Provide a sample of balanced diet. Have the student discuss the food that they eat with regard to the calorie content.	The students will be evaluated from their active participation in the class.
	Sugar (*gur*) Coke (soda water)	Give a lecture on the harmful effects of undesirable food : *e.g.*, spoiled vegetables which are sold at lower price can produce harmful effects in our body.	Ask the students to take their two day's food list and compare it with the list of foods in terms of vitamins.
		Most of us eat too much sugar (*gur*). Sugar has certain undesirable effects such as increasing tooth decay and reducing appetite for healthier foods. Much of material, besides sugar, in "soda water" (soft drink) is of doubtful value. Many of the flavours, acids and colouring matters are synthetic coal tar chemicals or extracts from plants which are not considered to be foods. Too much of any acid accelerates decay of teeth.	Make a report containing two columns. Head One – Food I must add to my diet. Head the other – undesirable foods I have eaten.
Problem V-E			
What is the effect of	Pictures of rats or persons eating	Exhibit the pictures of rats or persons eating unbalanced and poor diet. Give a lecture on the diseases caused	The students are asked to discuss the results of

Contd.

Contents	*Examples, Apparatus and Material*	*Activities*	*Evaluation*
poor diet?	poor diet.	by the poor diet, *e.g.*, knock knees, bow leg, small lower jaws, twisted teeth, anaemia.	poor diet at home and write a report in their notebooks.
		Guest Speaker	
		Invite a qualified doctor to explain the importance of balanced diet, harmful effects of eating spoiled vegetables and good living habits.	The students are asked to make a report on "Good living habits", giving their own examples, especially from their homes.
Problem V-F			
What is Chemotherapy?	Ayurvedic medicine "Chavan Prash" (health tonic) Kumaryasava (health tonic) Lavan Bhaskar Churn (powder to help digestion of food).	Give a lecture on chemotherapy. Emphasise the contributions made by the Indian Medical Science (Ayurveda) so as to develop confidence in Ayurvedic medicines which are mostly chemical compounds.	The students are asked to write a short essay on chemotherapy with particular reference to Ayurvedic medicines.
		Exhibit some of the most effective and patent Ayurvedic medicines which are generally used in villages.	
Problem V-G			
What is the	Some common patent	Have students list the patent medicines used in their	The students are asked to

Contd.

Contents	*Examples, Apparatus and Material*	*Activities*	*Evaluation*
nature of patent medicines?	medicines – Dettol (antiseptic) B.G. Phos (Tonic) Medicines prepared by unregistered medical practitioner	homes. Exhibit some common patent medicines such as laxatives. Have the students read the labels on some of the bottles and discuss their content. Critically examine the home made medicines given by unregistered medical practitioners in the village/town and elicit the following :	write a report on the disadvantages of home made medicines.
		These may contain harmful ingredients.	
		Some are habit forming	
		Dosage of such recommended medicines may not be correct as these doctors are unqualified.	
		The medicines may not have been prepared in a scientific manner.	
		These may be outdated.	
Summary Question		Round Table Conference	
What are good living habits?		Have the students discuss good living habits and contributions of science in improving our daily life.	The students will be evaluated from their active participation in the discussion and report to be written on good living habits.

Teaching Suggestions

This unit is designed to discuss the importance of science in our body development. To impart such type of knowledge is of great importance to the students in India, as in Indian villages very many unhealthy, non-hygienic habits are prevalent. The students should be helped to understand that eating is not only one of the most enjoyable activities, but it is also one of the most essential activities for body development. Choice of food determines the vitality, health and appearance of a man. Thus, food has more value than to provide pleasant tastes, although that in itself is important. Failure to eat a proper and balanced diet is to invite disease in the human body. (Most of the students especially in Indian villages are undernourished—while not eating enough good food). The teacher should discuss the importance of balanced diet and good living habits and harm caused by eating spoiled food. Spoiled vegetables are sold at very low rates in India. Due to poverty, poor people buy these spoiled vegetables without caring for the damage caused to their body.

The main purpose of including early medicine in this unit is to give importance to the contributions made by Indian doctors and Indian medical science so that students may build confidence in Ayurvedic medicines.

In the opinion of this writer, the teacher should discuss matters related to nature of patent medicines without going into too much technical detail. In a community, there are so many unqualified doctors (quacks) who prescribe home made medicines without having any proper medical knowledge. Sometimes these home made medicines prove fatal. The students should be made aware of disadvantages of the medicines prescribed by village quacks. The units discussed in this chapter may develop the competencies discussed earlier in a pupil at the primary and upper primary level in the context of Minimum Levels of Learning (MLLs).

However the following competencies may be developed from the above mentioned units (or other units to be developed by the participating teachers) at the primary level.

The Pupil

1. Acquires awareness about one's well-being in the context of social and natural environment;
2. Explores important aspects of one's socio-civic environment and comprehends their working;
3. Knows about various people at work and appreciates the importance about the 'world of work';
4. Understands and interprets the spatial and interactive relationship between man and his environment;
5. Begins to see the relationship between man's past and present, and to hold the past in its proper perspective;
6. Senses common but simple and easily observable socio-economic situations and problems, analyses them and seeks possible solutions at his level of experience;
7. Understands the factors contributing to preservation of good health;
8. Develops skill in gathering and classifying information about living things from the environment and drawing simple inferences.
9. Observes and examines some common characteristics of non-living things; and
10. Observes simple phenomena on the earth and in the sky and draws inferences.

References

1. John Brame, Fuels: Solid, Liquid and Gaseous (London: Arnold Publishing, 1955).
2. Arthur G. Hoff, Secondary School Science Teaching (Tornto: The Blackston Company, 1961).
3. P. Sinha, Pioneer General Science (Ambala : Gurdas Kapur and Sons, 1964)
4. UNESCO 1001 Science Experiments, (Paris: UNESCO, 1977).
5. R.M. Kalra, Meaningful Science Education for Rural School in India, New Delhi: Sterling Publishers, 1976.

VII

Environmental Studies and Integrated Science Teaching Activities and Projects

Sciences offers the possibility of far greater well being for the human race than has been known before.

Bertrand Russel
(The impact of science on society)

Suggested Environmental Studies Projects at the Elementary Level

The following are suggested Environmental Studies activities for the students which in-service teachers may like to consider in their actual classroom teaching learning situations.

1. Unit "Is our Air Polluted?" (General Outline)

1. Air is one of the most important things in our lives, we are going to see whether or not we breathe clean air and if not then what can be done about it?
2. Make a data table like, but not limited to, the one below. List the pollutants you found.

Data Table

Source of Pollutant	*Natural*	*Man Made*	*Harmful to People*
Car			
Bullock-Carts			
Tangas			
Sand storms			

3. Collect some old and some new magazines with pictures showing causes of air pollution. Cut them out and label them as to source.
4. Put the pictures in two stacks. In one stack, put the pictures which show natural pollution. In the other stack, put those which show man-made pollution.
5. How could air pollution be cut down in your community? (Civics)?
6. How does air pollution affect:
   (a) people,
   (b) birds?

2. *Unit on "Birds"*

1. The students may describe the birds in the locality emphasising common features and differences with reference to size, shape, weight, feathers, beaks, legs.
2. The students may be asked to classify birds with reference to features mentioned above.
3. Movement of birds may be discussed in respect of their movement in water, and in air.
4. Migration of birds may be discussed with special emphasis on weather conditions. The students may be asked to draw different kinds of birds (Art). They may be asked to discuss weather and seasons (Geography) relating to migration of birds.
5. Birds are useful to us in cleaning our environment and in pollination (Civics).
6. Birds live in communities. (Social Studies—Group living, sharing of food etc.).
7. Birds have different types of nests and are specific to the area (Geography).

3. *Unit on "Plants"*

1. There may be different types of plants in the community
2. Plants differ in size, shape, height but they have common system such as root, shoot, leaves, flowers, seeds etc.

3. Every part has a specific function.
4. Students may be asked to collect and preserve different kinds of leaves. Arrange different kinds of flowers artistically (Art).
5. Life is interdependent and we are indebted to plants for our existence (Social Studies). The following uses of plants may be discussed in detail.

Plants—Food for Man

1. Cereal, wheat, rice, corn.
2. Fruits such as mangoes, oranges and apples.
3. Vegetables such as carrots, potatoes, peas and spinach.
4. Sugar from sugarcane.

Plants—Food for domesticated animals

1. Grains, including corn, barley.
2. Root corps such as carrots.

Medicine from plants

1. Quinine from cinchona tree.
2. Opium from poppy plants.

Clothing from Plants

1. Linen from stems of flax.
2. Cotton from the cotton plant.

Fuel from Plants

1. Wood.
2. Petroleum.
3. Alcohol.

Uses of Plants to Man

Other benefits from Plants.

1. Rubber,
2. Lumber,
3. Dyes,
4. Perfumes.

4. *Does your family eat balanced diet?*

Maintain a record of quantities of food which you consume in your home. Note the value of each in terms of calories and compare with the Standard Diet Table. Find out whether your diet is a balanced diet or not. Repeat the above project with reference to other family members and keep a record.

5. *To study the difference between Pasteurised Milk and Impasteurised Milk*

Pour fresh cow's milk into four test tubes until each is about half full. Place cotton stoppers in two test tubes, leave the other tubes open. Place one stoppered and one unstoppered test tube in a large beaker containing hot water. Keep the temperature of water constant and stir the tubes gently. Remove the tubes from the water bath and keep these in a warm place with the other two test tubes. Note the condition of milk in each of the test tubes.

6. *To Investigate the Effect of Frost and Heat on Lumpy Soil.*

Take two hard lumps of clay moisten the lumps. Expose one hard lump to frost and the other lump to heat. Note the effect of these on lumps.

7. *To Study the Effect of Temperature on Rocks*

Take different kinds of rocks and heat them strongly in fire or in gas flame. Put them, one at a time, into cold water. Note the effect of the sudden change of temperature on the rocks. Explain why some of the rocks are affected more than others.

8. *To discover which of the following Soil types retain more moisture. Samples provided are (i) Sandy Soil (ii) Loam (iii) Clay (iv) Peat*

Take the above samples in air. Put cotton on each of the soil tubes to be used. Put exactly eight inches of soil into each tube, using sandy soil in one, loam in the second, clay in the third and peat in the fourth. Pack the soil lightly.

Invert each tube filled with soil over an empty water trough and pour exactly 100 ml. of water into it. Note the time required for the water pass through the soil, and the amount of water retained by the soil. Note the results.

Integrated Approach to Science Education Activities at the Elementary Level in Action

Integrated approach to science education at the elementary level has been discussed earlier. To justify the application of this approach, let us give an example. At the upper primary level (Classes VI-VIII), the topic concerning "preparation of soap", can be dealt with utilising integrated approach" in the following manner.

Preparation of Soap

Soap is prepared by boiling together Sodium Hydroxide and some vegetable oils or animal fat such as olive oil or cotton seed oil.

$$\text{Alkali—Fat} \rightarrow \text{Soap—Glycerine}$$

Apparatus: 40 grams of cotton seed oil; 10 grams of lye; beaker (1 L); water; thermometer; stirring rod; Bunsen burner.

Lab Instructions

To 40 grams of cotton seed oil, add 10 grams of lye in 20 ml of water. Pour the hot oil into the lye solution very slowly, stirring constantly and keeping the temperature under control especially below the boiling point. Heat it for about 30 minutes and then cool. Remove the soap formed and test its action in water.

Some Experiments about Soap

Have you ever wondered why soap and water cleans dirty hands better than just water alone? Have you ever asked "What is soap? What causes certain kinds of soap to float while other kinds cannot float?" or "Why does a house-wife get dishpan hands when she uses a detergent?"

Here are a few ideas to help guide your experimentation:

Don't be afraid to try your own ideas and to experiment in your own way.

1. Don't be discouraged if your questions aren't answered or if your experiment fails. Be sure to try again.
2. Ask the same question in different ways to answer the same question; and try different experiments.
3. Observe all of your experiments very carefully. Keep notes on what you do and how you do it.
4. Make use of yesterday's notes. These may contain the answers to today's questions.

Experiment 1—"Surface Tension"

Water has many properties—it is colourless, odourless, usually in a liquid form and has surface tension. What is tension? It is an ability to stop something from breaking through. Think of a line of children all holding hands. It is difficult to go through this line, but not impossible. Water molecules on the surface link together too. We call it surface tension. In this experiment, find out what soap does to surface tension.

Hints—First sprinkle some talcum powder on the water. Other materials you will find helpful are a needle, vegetable oil, bar of soap, liquid soap, and alcohol.

Questions

1. What does soap do to talcum powder that has been sprinkled on the surface of still water?
2. What happens at the tip of a needle (that has been coated with soap) when it is carefully brought to the surface of the water covered with talcum powder?
3. Is there a different effect if vegetable oil is rubbed on the needle instead of soap?
4. Does the temperature of water have any effect on what happens?

5. Does the amount of talcum powder used make any difference?
6. Will the needle float if soap is mixed with water before the needle is placed on the surface?
7. What will happen to a floating needle when a drop of liquid soap is carefully added to water?
8. Will salt have the same effect?
9. Does it matter to the floating needle if soap is mixed with water or just added to it?
10. What seems to be the effect on the surface tension if liquid soap is added to water? If alcohol is added or if the water is heated first.
11. What happens when a small piece of soap is placed on the bottom of a paper boat so that the soap touches the water?

Things to Do and Research

1. Explain with the help of a diagram, what surface tension is?
2. Show also, with the help of a diagram, how a needle is able to float on water.
3. Explain what soap does to surface tension.

Experiment 2—"Solubility"

When materials are able to dissolve in water, we say they are soluble in water. The amount that dissolve is called its solubility. Can soap dissolve in water? If it can, then we can experiment with its solubility—finding out if a little or a lot will dissolve in water, and what things can affect the amount that dissolves.

Some useful chemicals are a bar of soap, ammonia, detergent, vinegar, and salt.

Questions

1. How does the temperature of water in which the soap is placed affect the rate at which the soap dissolves?
2. Does stirring have any affect?

3. What is the effect on a piece of soap placed in warm water if ammonia is added to water?
4. Does the amount of ammonia make a difference on the effect that is produced?
5. Does the size of the piece of soap that is used make a difference in what is observed?
6. Does the same effect occur if detergent, instead of soap, is placed in warm water and ammonia is added?
7. How does adding vinegar to water affect the rate at which the dissolving soap dissolves?
8. Does salt affect the dissolving of soap in the same way as other chemicals do?
9. Will a piece of soap that has been placed in warm water dissolve at the same rate as an equal sized piece of soap that has been chopped into small bits and placed in the same amount of warm water?

Things to Do and Research

1. What is the chemical difference between "soap" and "detergent"?
2. Find out the meaning of "diffusion" and how it applies to this experiment?
3. Why does the amount of "exposed surface" cause bits of soap to dissolve differently than in bar form?

Experiment 3—"Sudsing"

Everyone is familiar with "suds". When we 'lather up' while washing, shaving, washing dishes, or laundry, we make suds. But everyone who has travelled a bit also knows you can't always 'lather up' in other parts of the country. In this experiment, you will find out why.

For this experiment all you need is bars of soap and different kinds of water—tap water, distilled water, sea water, and stream water (get the last two from your teacher), Try sudsing your soap with each of these.

Questions

1. Does the source of water have an effect on the amount of suds produced when the soap is mixed with water?
2. Does shaking the soap and water mixture have any effect?
3. Does it make any difference how much soap is used in each case?
4. What happens to the suds when the sudsing mixture is allowed to stand for a while—One hour? Overnight?
5. What difference do you find when you evaporate the distilled water and the sea water?
6. What happens when the material that is left from the boiled sea water is mixed with a soap suds mixture?

Things to Do and Research

1. Find out what soap suds really are.
2. Find out the difference between hard water and soft water, and where each is found.
3. Find out how distilled water is prepared.

Experiment 4—"The Density of Soap"

When we speak of density, we say that something is heavy or light for its size—a steel ball bearing is heavy for its size but a Styrofoam ball is light for its size. Can we also talk about soap in this way? Are some soaps heavy for their size and others light for their size?

To answer these questions, you will need a bar of soap—one of one make and another of a different make. You'll also need a tin cane and a fork. If the bars of soap are of different sizes, shave them until they are equal. Then put them in water.

Questions

1. Do both bars sink when placed in water? Would you say they have the same density?
2. Take half of the second bar and melt it. As it cools, beat it vigorously with a fork until it is solid. When cool, place it in water. Does it behave like the first soap or the other remaining part of the bar?

3. Take half of the first soap bar and melt it, but do not beat it when it is cooling. After cooling, place it in water. Which sample does it behave like?
4. Does the weight of a bar of soap change when it has been melted and beaten until cool?

Things to Do and Research

1. What are you doing with the second bar when you beat it while cooling it?
2. Find out the scientific meaning of the term 'density'.

Experiment 5—"Lubrication"

Most people know that when we lubricate things, like bicycles, we oil and grease them so that they run easier. Could soap be used instead? If so, should it be wet or dry? Thick or thin?

To answer these questions, try this experiment. Obtain a wooden board, three wooden blocks and a bar of soap. Rub the bottom of one block with dry soap, another with wet soap and leave the third one free of soap. Place the three blocks and the wet soap on one end of the board and tip it up. Watch what happens.

Questions

1. Which of the objects slide down the board faster?
2. How does the extent of slope of the board affect what occurs?

Things to Do and Research

1. Could strong soap solution be used to lubricate a bicycle?
2. Which is more slippery—a dry log or one covered with soap and suds?
3. Find out how lubricants work (*e.g.*, oil and grease)
4. Is soap and water a good lubricant?
   (*Hint*—can your hands slide over each other easily when washing?)
5. Find out why grease is sometimes used as a lubricant instead of oil.
6. Why isn't soapy water used as a lubricant for machines?
   (*Hint*—does the water evaporate?)

Experiment 6—"Bases"

Those people that have gotten soap into their eyes know what it feels like: It stings. Why does soap sting? Would detergent also sting if you got some in your eye?

To answer these questions, you will need a bar of soap, tea, a liquid called phenolphthalene solution, ammonia and vinegar.

See what effect you get by mixing each of the substances with the two test solutions—tea and phenolphthalene solution.

Hint—to the ones that have changed colour, add a few drops of vinegar.

Questions

1. Do all the samples do the same things to the test solutions? What kind of "reaction" do you see?
2. Do the test solutions react to the same or different samples? (*Hint*—watch the tea solution closely—the côlour change isn't very great.)
3. What happens to the colour of tea, if after adding soap, vinegar is added drop by drop?
4. Can the original colour of the tea be brought back if more vinegar is added?
5. Is vinegar an opposite to the other samples? (*Hint*—does it "undo" what the others do?)

Things to Do and Research

1. Find out why we call tea and phenolphthalene solutions as "indicators". What do they indicate?
2. What do ammonia and soap have in common?
3. Find out why soap helps to disinfect you when you wash.

Experiment 7—"Electrical Conductivity"

We all know some properties of metals; they are strong, resist burning, and conduct electricity (they are used in making wires). So we can say that metals have the property of electrical conductivity.

But are they the only ones that can conduct electricity? Can soap, possibly, conduct electricity too?

Find out by using a bar of soap, a dry cell, a flash light bulb and some wire. First, just use the wire to light up the bulb. The current will be travelling along the wires. Then rearrange things so that for the bulb to light up, the electricity must travel through the wire and the bar of soap like this. Then try liquid soap (or dissolve some bar soap in water) in place of the bar of soap.

Questions

1. Do the wire conduct electricity very well?
2. What is the substance in making of wire?
3. Must there be a "complete" path for electricity before the bulb will light up?
4. Will electricity go through the bar of soap?
(Does the bulb light up?)
5. Will electricity go through the liquid soap?, Soapy water?
6. Will "pure" water allow electricity to go through it?

Things to Do and Research

1. Find out what "electricity" really is.
(*Hint*—Read about electrons).
2. Compare how soapy liquids and metals are similar.
3. If water can't conduct electricity, why do people get electrocuted in bathtubs?
4. If you have the wire in the soapy liquid for a while, the electricity will eventually stop. Why?
(*Hint*—Do the wire get coated with a solid, cakey soap? Does this act to stop electricity flow?)

Experiment 8—"Viscosity of Soap"

The term "Viscosity" might be new to you. But new words are fun to learn—they're like a secret code that helps you talk about things much more easily. To learn about viscosity, you'll need 200ml. graduated cylinders, 2 marbles, some water, and some liquid soap (or shampoo). Observe what happens when you drop the marbles into each liquid at the same time.

Questions

1. Do both marbles fall at the same time?
2. Would you say that one of the liquids is "thicker" than the other?
3. Would you say that one of the liquids resist the marble's movement more than the other's?

Things to Do and Research

1. How would you connect the "thickness" of a liquid to its ability to 'resist' things going through it?
2. Would sugar syrup be more or less viscous than water?
3. Which liquid would pour more quickly—one with a high viscosity or the one with a low viscosity?
4. If you were the marble, what would you see happening as you feel through the water? Through the liquid soap?
5. If you place a bar of lead on top of a bar of gold, lead would "flow" into the gold after a few seconds. Does gold have a viscosity? It is high or low?

Experiment 9—"Emulsification"

Another new word: It may sound difficult, but the idea is really easy, as you will soon find out. Have you ever tried mixing olive oil with water? What happens if you add soap to this mixture? Try them and find out. Shake each solution vigorously, then let it stand.

Questions

1. Do olive oil and water mix? What seems to cause the problem?
2. Do olive oil and water mix if soap is added to the mixture?

Things to Do and Research

1. When two liquids are tried to mix together, and when they won't we, say they've been 'emulsified'. What does 'emulsify' mean?

2. Why won't oil and water mix by themselves?
(*Hint*—One of the liquids forms large drops?)

3. What does soap do to allow these liquids to mix?
(Does soap break up these large drops?)

4. Why is soap and water better than just water for cleaning your hands? (*Hint*—Does soap act as an emulsifying agent?)

Experiment 10—"Doming"

We all know what "domes" are—an upside down saucer is a dome., the top of a bubble is a dome, and the roof of a car is a dome (the light inside is called a dome light). Does the top of a liquid in a glass form a dome? Does water form "dome"? How does soap affect a liquid's "dome"? To find out, you'll need a cup, some water, an eye dropper, some liquid soap, mercury, and some salad oil. Fill a cup full of water but not overflowing. Observe the top surface. Then see how many drops of water can be added without overflowing. Observe the surface again. Try again, but add drops of liquid soap. Observe the surface of some mercury (look closely) and of some salad oil. Repeat the above steps for the salad oil but not for mercury.

Questions

1. Does plain water dome?
2. Can soapy water dome?
3. Does mercury dome better than water?
4. Does salad oil dome better than water?
5. Does the "thickness" of the liquid affect its doming?
6. Can you get more than a cup of water in a cup?

Things to Do and Research

1. Find out why doming happens.
(*Hint*—Does a liquid have surface tension?)

2. What does soap do to surface tension?
(*Hint*—does it get between the particles)

3. Why does doming happen better in a dry glass than in a wet glass?
4. Which liquid will pour faster—one that domes a lot or a little? Explain.

Experiment 11—"Capillarity"

If you have ever seen a thin piece of hollow glass tubing in water, you will have seen that the water rises up in it—higher than the surrounding water. This is because of capillary action. We call the glass tube, a capillary tube.

We can get this same action by wrapping a blotting paper of cheese or a paper towel over a glass of water so that one end is in the water. The question is—does soap have any affect on the capillary action of water? Let's find out.

In addition, you will need some liquid soap and olive oil. Try these as well as plain water and soapy water.

Questions

1. Does plain water have enough capillary action to drip from the cloth's end to the table?
2. Does adding soap to make soapy water help water's capillary action?
3. Does pure liquid soap have capillary action?
(*Note*: In all cases you must have patience—it may take a while)
4. How does the width of a paper towel or a blotting paper affect capillary action?
5. Do the same liquids that show capillary action also show a good ability to dome? A good ability to pour?

Things to Do and Research

1. You must have noticed that some liquids are able to "wet" the sides of their containers while others aren't. Find out how this is connected to capillary action.
2. Look at water in a test tube. The water's edges go up. The level around the water touching the test tube is called a meniscus. Draw what it looks like.

3. Explain why good doming liquids don't have good capillary action?
4. Why does soap in water increase the water's capillary action?

Experiment 12—"The Tyndell Effect"

Many scientists have things named after them that they discover. John Tyndell was a scientist who explained what happens when light is shone into a liquid with particles in it. Observe if you can see this effect. Does powdered soap in water reflect some light from a flashlight? If it does, you are watching the Tyndell effect.

Questions

1. What do you see when powdered soap is poured into clear water as you shine a flashlight through the side of a glass?
2. Does it make any difference if the water is hot or not?
3. Can you see the Tyndell effect by adding powdered soap to olive oil?

Things to Do and Research

1. Explain how reflection is important in the Tyndell effect.
2. Why will the Tyndell effect disappear when the soap dissolves? (*Hint*—Do the soap particles become smaller?)

VIII

Motivational Devices in Science Teaching Learning

> The first duty to children is to make them happy. The first essential of a child's preparation for life should be the formation of cheerful habit by training its mind towards sunshine, developing every possibility of the cheerful faculties. —*Sir Thomas Buxton*

A student's interest is aroused only when he sees a real use of what he is studying and when it satisfies some felt need and provides some value he accepts.

Accordingly, teachers must provide the environment which afford both—experiences desired by the student, as well as a basis for the formal educational goals of the schools.

To motivate students, an activity is required that takes them out of the classroom atmosphere, and which seems to them, at least, to be a non-school and fun activity.

To achieve the above objectives, the following activities are suggested:

1. Science Fair
2. Improvisation of apparatus of teaching of science
3. Academic games in science teaching

1. Science Fair

The science fair might be divided into various booths. For Example:

Booth I—*What is the chemistry of building material?*

The students should exhibit the common chemical substances used in building materials, *e.g.*, cement, lime, plaster. The student should exhibit insulating material and explain the use of this material to present the loss of heat in winter.

Booth II—How can we make our village drinking water potable?

The students should show drinking water under microscope and should explain various methods of purification. The students should emphasise that drinking water should be sedimented and boiled.

Booth III—What is balanced diet?

The student should explain about balanced diet and disadvantages of taking poor diet with the help of pictures of rats or persons eating poor diet.

Booth IV—How can we dispose human waste effectively?

Have the students explain the effective method of disposal of human waste in the village by digging ditches and dumping the human waste in these ditches and covering with lye. This would reduce the number of flies which are a source of many diseases.

Booth V—How to remove spot and stains from the clothes?

Have the students bring the clothes from the home which have stains of ink, rust, paint and grease. They should remove these spots with the help of organic solvents such as benzene, alcohol, acetone and carbon tetrachloride.

Booth VI—What are pesticides, antiseptics and disinfectants?

The students should explain the uses of these chemical substances with some concrete examples. For example, pesticides are used in killing mosquitoes which are harmful for mankind.

Booth VII—How can we manufacture soap?

The students prepare a simple soap by heating animals and vegetable fats or oil in a boiling solution of sodium hydroxide.

Booth VII—Some interesting scientific demonstrations.

(i) Cracker deluxe

Equipment:

1 Ring stand with ring (small)	1 Asbestos sheet 3′ × 3′
1 Large metal container (such as roasting pan)	1 Paper cup
1 Pair of goggles, or protective glasses	1 Graduated cylinder
5 ml glycerine	10 Grams Potassium permanganate

Precautions:

1. Avoid spilling or touching Potassium Permanganate; it stains hands and clothes.
2. Keep all students six feet away. They won't miss a thing except they fallout.
3. Have room well ventilated.

Method:

1. Assemble stand and ring. Place in roaster.
2. Put asbestos sheet on table.
3. Put roaster in the middle. Put cup in the ring.
4. Measure Potassium Permanganate and put in the cup.
5. Measure glycerine and add it to Potassium Permanganate.
6. Stir briefly with a glass rod–until mixed.
7. Stand back

(ii) Cake (Christmas/Diwali)

Equipment:

1 Half cup granulated sugar	50 ml concentrated Sulphuric Acid
1 Sheet of Asbestos at least one square.	1-100 ml graduated cylinder, goggles or protective glasses
1 Beaker (100 ml)	

Precautions:

1. Use extreme caution in measuring and pouring acid.
2. Keep all students at least six feet away.
3. Allow 'cake' to cool. Put it in incinerator with due caution

Method:

1. Measure sugar into beaker.
2. Place beaker in middle of asbestos.
3. Slowly pour acid into sugar.
4. Stand back and watch the 'cake' rise.

(iii) Volcano

Equipment:

1 Ring stand with ring

1 Asbestos gauze square

1 Evaporating dish

1 Bunsen burner

1 Newspaper to cover 3′ × 3′ square

Foil to cover newspaper

Ammonium Dichromate (about 15 grams depending on size of evaporating dish)

1 Pair of protective glasses or goggles

Precautions:

1. Good ventilation.
2. No student within six feet.

Method:

1. Cover table with newspaper, then foil.
2. Place ring stand assembly in the middle.
3. Put Asbestos gauze on ring.
4. Put measured amount of Ammonium Dichromate in the evaporating dish. Place it on asbestos gauze.

5. Light Bunsen burner or spirit lamp.
6. Put on the goggles.
7. Hold burner under wire gauze, moving it to heat all portion.
8. When the action starts, remove burner, turn off the gas, and stand back to enjoy the show.

(iv) Christmas Bobble from the Kitchen

Equipment:

Two tall fat beer glasses or ordinary white vinegar three teaspoons per glass, red food colouring.

Tap water to fill baking soda, 6 mothballs per glass, green food colouring.

Method:

1. Fill glasses with water.
2. Slowly stir at least three teaspoons of vinegar into each glass, then two teaspoons of baking soda.
3. Drop six mothballs into each glass.
4. Add vegetable dye.
5. Balls will first sink then, one after another, begin bouncing up and down.

(v) Colour Television (Old Massau Experiment)

Equipment:

1. Solution A-15 g of Potassium Iodate in 1,000ml of water.
2. Solution B-4 g of soluble starch in 500 ml of boiling water.
3. Solution C-3 g of Mercuric Chloride ($HgCl_2$) in 1,000 ml of water.
4. Ring stand assembly, asbestos gauze, and Bunsen burner.

Method:

1. Make solutions A and C.
2. For solution B, make a starch paste in a small amount of cold water. Heat the water in beaker over a Bunsen burner or a spirit

lamp. As it nears boiling, add starch. Boil for a minute, then remove flame and allow it to cool.

3. At the time of the demonstration, mix equal amount of solutions B,C and A in that order, in a 500 ml beaker. The solution will first turn bright orange, then blue-black.

(vi) Blushing Rose

Equipment:

One paint brush of ½″ size	One paint brush of 1″ size
Solution of Phenolphthalein	50 ml (denatured Ethyl alcohol)
One tack board	100 ml Ammonia solution
One sponge	50 ml water

Method:

1. Before class, have a pupil draw the outline of a rose (about 18″). Mount on tack board.
2. With appropriate brushes, paint the rose with phenolphthalein, Alcohol, water mixture. Allow it to dry.
3. Just before the demonstration, dampen the rose lightly—a very fine spray works well.
4. Have a sponge out of sight soaking in ammonia.
5. Squeeze out sponge, and hold near the painted rose. When Ammonia has evaporated, the blush will disappear.

(vii) Frying of Paper in Paper Can

Make a can of paper. Add mustard oil in the paper can. Heat the paper can with a spirit lamp and put paper in it. Paper does not catch fire because heat is transmitted to paper by convection currents. Firstly the oil is heated and then heat is transmitted by convection currents.

2. Improvisation of Apparatuses for Teaching of Science

In a developing country, general economy does not permit physical equipment for explaining and demonstrating all concepts of science teaching to be bought from the market. It does not take a scale to know that one was able to move an object with a block-and-tackle. One's senses provide often sufficient instrumentation, and perhaps the most appropriate under the circumstances. In fact simplicity of approach needs to be encouraged.

The following activities exemplify importance of home-made apparatuses in science teaching.

Activity I—Interaction of Sea water with Metals

Sea water and soil contain various salts including Sodium Chloride. These salts interact with metals that are in contact with each other and with the water or soil. A demonstration of the kind of action that can occur is given by the following activity.

Place four dry cells in series and connect copper wires to them. Put the other ends of the Copper wire into some salt water. Make note of the appearance of the salt solution and the shape of the wires before and after the reaction starts.

Find out what has happened to the salt solution and to the copper wire. The reaction will take a while. You might try using a toy train transformer instead of a battery and note the difference.

Activity II—Setting up an Aquarium

Set up an aquarium tank using an underground filter. Discuss in class how the air bubbles rising in the tube pump the water from under the gravel.

Activity III—Floatation of Materials

It is interesting that floating docks and even ships can be made of concrete. Artificial clay (plasticene) is an excellent material to use in demonstrating floatation of materials denser than water.

Completely cover a match box with plasticene and then put it in water. Try explaining why it floats. Next try making small boats of plasticene. See who can make a boat that supports the largest number of paper clips. Each student should be given the same weight of plasticene.

Activity IV—Block-and-Tackle—A Pulley System

Lifting heavy weights is frequently involved even in skilled trades. A block-and-tackle is an important tool necessary for the safety of the worker. In block-and-tackle, the important feature is the number of strands of rope that are actually physically supporting the object to be lifted.

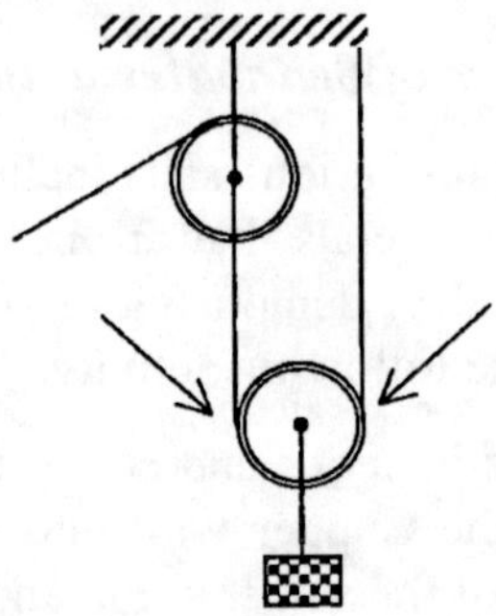

Figure 1. Two strands support the weight, thus the force you exert is one-half the weight of the object lifted.

In the above example, two strands of rope physically support the object to be lifted. Obtain a real block-and-tackle such as frequently used by hunters to lift a moase carcass for cleaning and skinning. Change the number of strands of rope supporting a weight and see how this affects the force you have to exert.

Activity V: Proper Use of Materials in Supporting Weight

Different materials have different abilities to support weight. Your safety in work depends on proper use of materials.

1. Set up two buckets, one supported by a number 16 copper wire and the other by a number 16 iron wire. Add sand, one kg. at a time, to both buckets recording the height from the floor of the buckets each time. Which metal is stronger?
2. Obtain 1″ × 4″ boards 6 feet long, one each of Hemlock, Cedar and Pine. Support each, one inch from the end and have each support a bucket by its handle. Use the same

procedure as above. Have a discussion on the importance of using the kind of wood specified by engineers and architects.

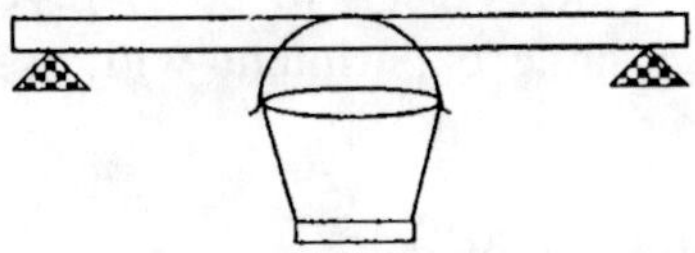

Figure. 2

Activity VI—Guest Speaker (Demonstration)

Invite a repair mechanic of small gasoline engines, such as are used in lawn mowers, to bring to class a four stroke cycle engine and take apart, explain the function of all parts and put it back together.

Activity VII—Dry Cell Economy

Buy two samples each of the cheapest and the most expensive carbon-zinc "D" size dry cells and two of the same size "Alkaline" cells. You will also need six number 222 bulbs. Connect each cell to a lamp bulb for half an hour at a time with at least two hours rest time in between connected times. Keep track of the time for each cell and make note of how bright the lamp bulb shines. You could use a third Alkaline cell and lamp that is used for only a couple of minutes at a time as a comparison standard. When the lamps are ably dimmer, make special note of that fact.

Make a decision regarding the useable life for each of the different kinds of cells, then decide what the cost per hour is for each kind. Do the cells live up to the manufacturer's claims?

Activity VIII—Lamp Bulb Economy

The manufacturers of house-hold lamp bulbs are now showing the life expectancy for their product on the carton. A typical life expectancy is 1000 hours. Set up a circuit for lighting three lamps of the same wattage rating (for instance 40 watts). Record the date and hour when the test is started and let the lamps run day and night until they burn out. How many days did they burn?

If a bulb burns out during the night, when you are not there to record the time, how much error will be involved in your data and conclusions? Try the same experiment with some lamp bulbs for which the life time is not stated.

How much did the test cost?

Be sure to start this test early in the school year.

Activity IX: Electric Motors

Request a local electric motor repair shop that they bring to the class examples of the following kinds of electric motors: split phase, capacitor, repulsion induction, 3 phase, universal, direct current.

The characteristics, car and special uses of each should be explained.

3. Academic Games in Science Teaching

One of the most satisfying experiences a science teacher can have is to see the gleam of desire to learn in the eyes of a highly motivated pupil. Intelligent and pointed questions that show a pupil really cares about science is the response every science teacher desires.

A few boys and girls are highly motivated but no matter how the teacher varies his classroom technique, some pupils still stare out of the window. Of course, some of them lack the capacity for work. It is however, the pupil who has the ability to work, yet shows no interest, represents the real challenge to the dedicated science teacher. The above type of student generally experiences the threat of failure which has a negative effect on him (the pupil), resulting in a dislike for the subject. This writer's experience in some developing and developed countries (especially in rural, tribal, hilly and slum areas) indicates that pupils, especially in a science class, stayed away from the class, sometimes from school, because they were "afraid of teachers". "They did not want to be ridiculed" and they "just didn't like the school". When asked what they feared, pupils

responded that they feared being brought to the attention of the class or yelled at.

Major Contributing Factors for Student's Lack of Interest in Science

In order to remedy this negative attitude of our pupils towards a science class and school on the whole; one must analyse the most important contributing factors for the above situation. In addition to lack of meaningful science education experiences for the above pupils, the writer believes that the major fault lies with science teaching because they have endorsed and practised only conventional methods of teaching and learning science. That these pupils need individual recognition and attention is quite apparent. We have to motivate these pupils and make them "Interested" in learning science.

To motivate a pupil to learn science, the writer contends that the environment may include innovative teaching learning and evaluation strategies in science for the pupils at the secondary level. These innovative educational endeavours may be in the form of activities which takes them out of the classroom atmosphere, and which seem to them at least, to be a non school activity and remove from them fear and threat of a failure by the science teacher.

Academic Games as Innovative Teaching Aids

Most of the pupils play a number of games such as snakes and ladders and guessing games with various versions. These games sometimes become more nearly a source of pleasure to the pupil than a source of boredom or burden, instilling in him a desire to learn. Thus the threat of failure is reduced and that of motivation increased. Success is very likely to result when interest is aroused. Development of interest and motivating the pupils to do quality work should be the responsibility of science educators. We should make sincere efforts to motivate our pupils in developing countries by providing educational experiences to them which are interesting and meaningful. In order to achieve the above objective, the writer in this book suggests some innovative teaching aids in the form of scientific games "for learning science without a teacher". It is worthwhile to mention here that there may be science learning without a science teacher but it may not be true to assume that an effective science teaching may take place without a teacher. The above mentioned scientific games may serve as an additional aid to provide pupils a fundamental knowledge and arouse their interest in science. Thus, the emphasis is on learning science with the help of these games and evaluation becomes an important part and parcel of the gamut of learning.

Self-Evaluation and Academic Games in Science Learning and Teaching

In these games, pupils may be given opportunities to develop the concept of self-evaluation. Stress is to be put on helping pupils learn to think, to develop fresh meanings for themselves, to examine possibilities and to create new combinations from original or available data. That is to say, evaluation becomes a part of teaching.

Furthermore, the process of self-evaluation must provide feedback to pupils so that they can learn better and change their behaviour. Evaluation should measure individual pupils achievement with a traditional "bell shaped curve standard", or with the achievement of other pupils. The most important outcome of self-evaluation is fostering the development of a positive self concept for each student. In most developing countries, it is quite common that poor student's failure, especially in rural high schools in science, is due to unhealthy perception of the self and the world. We must help a pupil to develop his positive self image and to achieve this we can help him to meet the challenge of getting the realistic and attainable goals of science education. Furthermore, evaluation system must recognise the pupil to be appreciated for which he is and for what he has the potential to become.

The above discussion suggests that the academic games, having the concept of self evaluation as a component, may be good learning material, for it helps eliminate the obstacles in learning science. In order to justify the above condition, the following academic games in science teaching have been developed by the author and have been quite helpful in motivating pupils in science education especially with chemistry subject:

1. Snakes and ladders game,
2. Guessing game—the chemical charade,
3. Science password.

Snakes and Ladders Game

Game in Action:

Material Required (i) Snakes and Ladders Chart which is an outline of the periodic table, (ii) Two sets of cards (a) white (b) Pink

Each card contains a question.

Version I—A game for two or more players

1. Each player chooses a 'man' of a different colour which will be moved along the given 'snakes and ladders' chart. The first player to reach number 107 will be the winner.
2. Order of players in the game is decided by a dice. In the event that two players are involved in the game, the first player may be chosen by a coin toss.
3. The cards are shuffled and turned face down in a pile.
4. To start the game, the first player (let us say A the questioner) takes the top card from the white cards deck and reads the question to the person on his left (or to his opponent Player B—to answerer, if there are only two players.) After the answer is given correctly by the player B, the answerer moves his 'man' to the appropriate number of places on the 'snakes and ladders' chart according to the marks allotted for the question. The number of points a player moves his man in one turn, is indicated on the question card *e.g.* if the answerer attempts the question correctly worth two marks, the answerer will move his 'man' by two positions on the chart. If the answerer (Player B) does not answer the question correctly, he is not allowed to move his man, and the card is replaced at the bottom of the deck.
5. Now the player B picks up the next card from the top of the white deck and reads the question to the player A. (now-the

answerer), if there are two players, (or to the third player), and follows the procedure outline in step 4.

6. The players take their turn and the game continues.
7. When a player's 'man' reaches a number on the 'snakes and ladders' chart where he has to climb the ladder, the questioner picks up a card from the pink deck and reads the question to the answerer. If the answerer answers the question correctly, he would be allowed to climb the ladder, otherwise he stays put (where he is).
8. When a player's man reaches a snake mouth, he can be saved from the 'bite' by answering the question correctly from the pink card deck picked by the questioner. If the answerer cannot answer the question correctly, his man is moved to the position (downward) indicated by the snake tail.
9. The player who reaches number 107 first is the number one winner. Others would continue till they finish the game.

Version II—Solitaire (Game played by an individual)

1. The cards are thoroughly shuffled and turned face down.
2. To start the game, the player must answer a question from the white cards deck. Unless he answers the question correctly, he cannot move his man to the number position.
3. The player picks the top card, places it in the solitaire folder to conceal the answer and turns the card over.
4. He scores himself and moves his man accordingly.
5. Cards are not returned to the desk.
6. When a player's man reaches a number on the 'snakes and ladders' chart where he has to climb the ladder, he must pick up a card from the pink deck and answer the question. If he answers the question correctly, he climbs the ladder. *i.e.*, by moving his man to a higher number where the ladder leads him), otherwise he stays put (where he is).
7. When a player's man reaches a snakes mouth, he can be saved from the 'bite' by answering the question from the pink card. If he cannot answer the question correctly, his

man is moved to the position downwards indicated by the snake tail.

8. The player finishes the same successfully, if he reaches number 103.

Version III—An additional option (Bonus and Penalty points)

At the beginning of the game, the players must decide if they wish to include this feature in the game. Bonus and Penalty points is an extra feature which helps the answerer from the snake bite by giving him another chance in addition to his failure to answer the question from the pink deck. The other rules remain the same as that of version I.

Academic Games in Chemistry Teaching

(a) Chemical 'Snakes and Ladders' Game[1]

This game is played on an outline sketch of the periodic table. Two or more than two students can play this game. If desired, the game can also be played as solitaire (individualised).

Material Required

Snakes and Ladders Chart which is an outline of the Periodic table.

Two sets of cards: (a) White cards deck, (b) Pink cards deck.

Each card contains a question and its answer in the following manner:

Determine the weight in grams of the following compound (use atomic weights given in the periodic table): One molecule of Na_2SO_4.[Ans : 142 g]

Penalty: One mark of the incorrect units.

Bonus: One mark for showing the complete work.

1. White cards contain questions based on chemical facts.
2. Pink cards contain "difficult" questions based on comprehension and application of chemical knowledge in daily life.

3. Some cards having bonus and penalty point (For version III of the game).
4. A 'Man' of different colours.
5. Solitaire folder is a card holder which has been designed to conceal the answer. (For version II of the game).

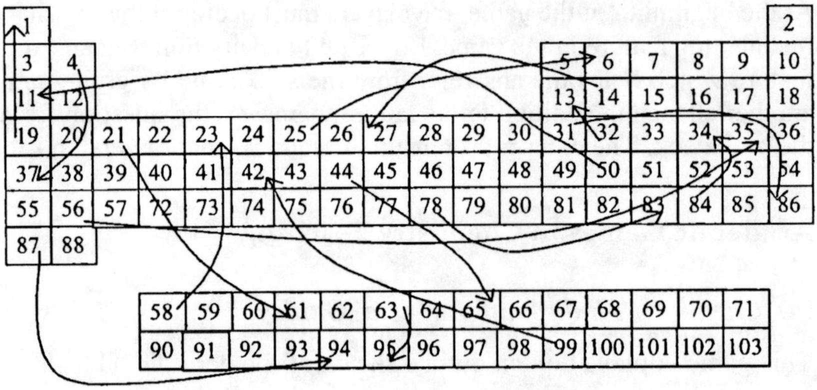

Figure 3: (Periodic Ups and Downs)

Define Chemistry? (White Card)

Answer:

It is the study of the identification, characterisation and transformation of substances. OR (*1 mark*)

1. Chemistry deals with the study of elements.
2. What information is contained in a chemical formula? (White Card)

Answer

(i) The elements present in the substance. (*1 mark*)

(ii) The number of atoms of each element in a molecule of the substance. (*1 mark*)

Using the atomic weights listed in your periodic table, determine the weights in grams of : (Pink Card)

(a) 0.10 mole of Na_2SO_4; (b) 2.0 moles of CO_2

Answer:

(a) 14 kg (*1 mark*)

(b) 88.0 g (*1 mark*)

Penalty: for incorrect or missing units (*1 mark*) for the incorrect number of significant figures. (White Card) (*1 mark*)

Define Charle's Law

Answer: The volume of a gas sample is prepositional to the absolute temperature provided that the pressure is kept constant. Bonus: V/T = Constant or V=KT (if pressure is constant).

Snakes and Ladders Game in Physics and Biology Teaching

In India and in other developing countries, science is taught as an integrated subject comprising of Chemistry, Physics and Biology at the elementary level. Thus, for imparting meaningful science education to our pupils at the secondary level in developing countries, the writer had developed snakes and ladders game in Physics and Biology. A few samples of this game are given below.

Physics Snakes and Ladders Game.

This game is played on an outline sketch of the snakes and ladders chart. All the other requirements and rules of the games are exactly similar to the Chemical Snakes and Ladders Game.

Questions relating to Physics are again available in white and pink cards.

1. Which of the following is a fundamental quantity? (White Card)

   (a) Velocity (b) Volume

   (c) Area (d) Length

   Answer : (a) (*1 mark*)

2. Force is given by the relation—(White Card)

   (a) Momentum/acceleration (b) Work/distance

   (c) Energy/time

   Answer: (B) (*1 mark*)

3. What is the correct unit for measuring astronomical distances? (White Card)

   (a) Centimetre (b) Kilometre

   (c) Light Year (d) Angstrom Unit

   Answer: (b) *(1 mark)*

4. One of the flagellated protozoans is : (White Card)

   (a) Amoeba (b) Entamoeba

   (c) Polystomolla (d) Englona

   Answer: (d) *(1 mark)*

5. Endocrine glands pour their secretion into the (White Card)

   (a) Oxygenated blood (b) Deoxygenated blood

   (c) Rontal portal vein (d) Hopatic portal vein

   Answer: (b) *(1 mark)*

6. When male and female gametes differing only in one character are crossed it is called a : (White Card)

   (a) Monohybrid (b) Dihybrid

   (c) Polyhybrid

   Answer: (a) *(1 mark)*

(b) Guessing Game—The Chemical Charade

Version I: Game in Action

The whole class is divided into two groups. One pupil from each group is picked up (by a democratic process such as voting etc.) to act as a leader of their respective groups. One pupil from the class is agreed upon to act as the master of the game and the other as the score-keeper. The score-keeper of the game draws a line on the black board to divide it in two parts, one for team 'A' and one for team 'B'. The master of the game has a deck of cards, which he shuffles and puts on the table. He explains the rules of the game to the two groups.

1. A toss of the coin decides which team would start the game. Let us suppose team 'A' wins the toss an 'actor' from team 'A' will come to the front and the rest of the team 'A' will do the guessing work.
2. The actor picks up a card from this pack and gets 15 seconds to think.
3. The actor will give clues to his team by gestures or by drawing diagrams on the black board.
4. Only team 'A' who has sent the actor to the front will ask questions which will be answered by 'yes' or 'no' by the actor. The team is allowed to ask any question that may be answered by 'yes' or 'no'.

Although this actor is not allowed to speak at all, the pupil audience is permitted to query him. (The other rules remain the same as that of Version I of this game).

For example:

1. How many words are there in the substance?
   (The actor reveals the number by holding up the appropriate number of fingers).
2. How many letters are there in the substance?
   (Again the number is indicated by raising the correct number of fingers).
3. Is it an element or a compound? (The actor points to the periodic table to indicate an element)
4. Is it a solid? (The actor points to be bench)
5. Is it a liquid? (He indicates the tap)
6. Is it a gas? (He waves his hand in the air)

The designated actor may indicate properties of compounds under study by demonstration. Meanwhile the class is writing the guessed elements and their properties with their uses in their note books without referring to previous notes. Score: One mark for each correct answer entered in the card.

One additional mark for the chemistry or chemical equation involved in the gaseous element.

Each pupil, in turn, becomes an 'actor'.

Science Password

Equipment :

1. "A" card(s) containing one-half of a clue of a chemical definition.
2. "B" card(s) containing the complementing half of the definition given in "A" card.
3. Two holders to contain the cards.
4. A scoring dial containing numbers one to ten and a moveable pointer.

Organisation

The class is divided into two teams "A" and "B", and arranged in pairs with an opposing partner. (In this way each student participates)

Object of the Game

To guess the correct "password" from a chemical definition or clue presented by an opponent partner. (The "A" and "B" members of the opponent pairs alternately "give" and "receive" clue words, contained in a holder to prevent the opposing partner from viewing the correct response).

Procedure

1. The initiating "A" player places the pointer of the scoring dial at 10. He then gives a clue word to his partner.
2. If the "B" player fails to make the correct password response after this first clue, the pointer of the dial is moved to 9 and the turn goes to the opposing "A" player who now supplies a clue to his "B" player. As long as the "password" remains unguessed, the turn is passed between alternating "A" and "B" partners.
3. When a player finally guesses the correct password, he scores the point value on the dial indicated by the pointer. For example if two clue words have been released without a successful "password" response, the point value for the correctly guessed third clue word is 8.

4. If after ten clues, however (5 given by each player) the password has still not been supplied, no "B" player scores for that word.

Some examples of chemical passwords:

Card "A" *Card "B"*

Ion Electrically charged particles *e.g.* K^+, $Al^{+3}Cl^-$

Temperature: Represents degree of hotness or coldness.

Formula : Represents a molecule of a compound, *e.g.*, H_2O, $CuSO_4$.

Molarity: The molarity of a solution is the number of moles of solute per litre of solution and is usually designated by M.

Conclusion: The writer contends that we, as science educators, may stress upon the pupils (with actual examples) about learning science as a pleasant endeavour rather than memorisation of certain isolated scientific principles.

Hopefully, this approach may motivate a pupil to learn science and has lot of ramifications in implementation of learning process in elementary science education.

Reference

1 This game is an outcome of this author's (as a project Director-cum-author) UNESCO Project.

IX

Development of Scientific Temper

> If civilisation is to survive, we must cultivate the science of human relationships—the ability of all people of all kinds, to live together, in the same world at peace.
>
> —*Franklin D. Roosevelt*

Science in democratic societies benefits all people, and we must ensure that they become aware of the advantages which science can bring to their lives. Economic and technical growth, accrues to a society in proportion to the effectiveness with which it uses its scientific talent. Before it is too late, we must prepare our younger generation to assume the responsibility of understanding the social, cultural, economical and technical aspects of science.

Scientific Temper—What is it?

From operational point of view, scientific temper may be defined as a value frame, an outlook for the world and an approach to one's world of deed and action. Thus, scientific temper is a value as well as a method of attaining human rights in terms of humanism.

Nehru describes the concept of a scientific temper as follows in a very lucid manner.

"A person who cannot understand another's view point is to that extent limited in mind and culture, because nobody can presume to have the fullest knowledge and wisdom or truth. If we shut our minds to that then we not only deprive ourselves of it but we cultivate an attitude of mind which is opposed to that of uncultured man... . An open mind has scientific approach to life's problems.

The above conviction is also substantiated by Gautam Budha in the following statement:

> *"Believe nothing*
> *Merely because you have been told it*
> *Or because you yourself have imagined it*
> *Do not believe that your teacher tells you,*
> *merely out of respect for the teacher*
> *But whatever after due examination and analysis*
> *You find to be conducive to be the good,*
> *the benefit, the welfare of all things,*
> *That doctrine believe and cling to,*
> *and take it as your guide"*
>
> *—Lord Budha*

Rane Descartes in his Discourse of Method aptly substantiated the above conviction.

"I learned not to believe too firmly those things which I had been persuaded to accept by example and custom only; and in this way I freed myself gradually from many errors which obscure the natural light of our understanding and render us less capable of reasons".

How do we Inculcate Scientific Temper?

Scientific temper is basically open mindedness, a desire to have accurate knowledge and use of verified knowledge for solution of problems. In this context, it is imperative to define the term "Science". According to the Columbia Encyclopaedia, science is defined as "an accumulated and systematised learning in science which in general sense is restricted to natural phenomena. The progress of science is marked not only by an accumulation of facts, but by the emergence of scientific method and of the scientific attitude."

From the above definition, three basic ingredients of science can be identified

1. An accumulated and systematised knowledge of environment,
2. Scientific method; and
3. Scientific method of inquiry.

The first ingredient indicates the Product of Science, while the second and the third ingredients indicate the Process of Science.

The product of science is truth like Everest, which is accumulated by the ordering of scientific information (facts) gathered by the scientists.

It will be unjust if we say that science is organised knowledge for there is an equally significant aspect namely the modes of acquiring knowledge which is dealt in the process of science. It is nothing but the process of observation, experimentation and logical interpretation. It involves the basic language of science. It responds to unlimited queries in a Systematic Manner. Science as a process is an attempt to order the facts of observations to represent them in some coherent systematic way in an articulate structure of a language. Thus much of the science begins when observations leaves off and much of the science concerns what goes on before observations begin. The key to the process approach of gaining knowledge is scientific method. Though through times different scientists have moulded this scientific temper according to their own ways. In these ways there has been a common denominator which provides the pattern of thinking and working. The scientific way of thinking is a natural outcome of a scientific temper. The wonders of nature are as delightful for a scientist as the building blocks to a young child, who forms various shapes out of these, breaks them and again discovers new ways of making new shapes. This may be included as one of the ingredients of scientific temper. The following ingredients of scientific temper have been adapted from various eminent science education readings.

Ingredients of Scientific Temper

Scientific Inquiry

This very first ingredient of scientific temper involves sheer joy of discovery which has been aptly described in the following paragraph:

> "Anyone who has ever worked in any science knows how much aesthetic joy he has obtained. That is, in the actual activity of science, in the process of making a discovery, however humble it is, one cannot help feeling an awareness of beauty."

Thus it can be said that the real crux of scientific enquiry lies in asking questions and providing answers to them.

The Sense of Humility

Scientist is a normal human being possessing scientific temper. There never had been a great scientist who did not make bold guesses, and, there never was a bold man whose guesses were not sometimes wild. Newton was wrong, in the setting of his time, to think that light is made up of particles. Faraday faulted when he looked in his setting for a link between Electro-magnetism and gravitation. Scientific temper gives rise to the spirit of humility. It makes one free of pride and arrogance. It bids ado to rigidity, dogmatism and categorical attitude. Thus scientific findings are tentative and not rigid.

Scientific Findings are Tentative

Science is a human enterprise with its own limitations. The whole process of the scientific enterprise is continuously replenished by new facts and discoveries. The body of knowledge of the scientific information derived from scientific findings can be compared to a wall made of bricks. The bricks are like scientific facts which are renewable and replaceable—weaker ones by stronger ones without damaging the structure of the wall. The perseverance of every individual is different—a woman is looked by her child as a mother, by her brother as a sister and by her husband as his wife. Each scientist looks at the same problem in a different way. As a result, sometimes the whole edifice of scientific knowledge stumbles down and more reliable scientific information takes its place. It so happened when Nicholas Copernicus revolutionised the existing knowledge by establishing that the sun, rather than earth, is the centre of solar system. With time his ideas were further corrected, modified and enlarged by Galileo, Kepler and Newton. Thus in the process of discovery, scientific findings are tentative and some scope of failure of some ideas is there. Dealing with these failures is the next ingredient of scientific temper.

Positive Approach to Failure

Human search and research is learning by steps of which none is final and the mistakes of generation are rungs in the ladder no less than their correction by the next. Acceptance of failure to the success which can be proved by the examples of Dr. Paul Ehrilock (1908), a Nobel Prize Winner in Medicine and Philosophy, and Howard Rogers. Dr. Paul Ehrilock experienced 605 failures which contributed positively to the development of 606th formula in the domain of medical research. Howard Rogers, a Chemist, spent 15 years and took 500 different compounds before he could invent a new chemical molecule which was needed for developing in sixty seconds instant colour pictures.

Thus failures help the scientist to reconstruct his intellectual atmosphere and enable him to control his emotions during the process of investigation which is the next ingredient of scientific temper.

Control of Emotions

It is an acknowledged fact that scientific temper help scientists to tackle problems of failure, tolerance and prejudices. He is more careful, patient, devoted, courageous and open minded. He uses truth in procedure and in reporting. He takes failures in his stride and keeps his guns ready to fire out at new targets. James Brijant Covant mentions the stumbling ways in which even the ablest of the early scientists had to find through thickest of erroneous observations misleading generalities, inadequate formulations and uncertain predictions.

Scientists are human beings with emotions and weaknesses but well guarded by scientific temper that they should possess. Chance plays an important role in their lives especially in scientific discoveries. Galivani and Voltas worked on electricity and while working on the original problem, it was by chance that Voltas discovered that even without frogs, the moist material would give the same results. Louis Pasteur further gave chance its right place by stating that chance favours only the prepared mind which is the next ingredient of the scientific temper.

Scientific Temper and the Prepared Mind

The factor of chance plays an important role in the prepared mind. Scientific temper keeps the mind prepared by developing a scientific attitude towards the problem. Prepared mind is not just the monopoly of scientists but every educated person can possess the same. Common sense is again an essential feature of any endeavour. Oliver Wendell Holiness attaches such an importance to it that he feels that scientific temper can be compared to a furniture of the upper floor only if he has common sense on the ground floor.

Though there is no single scientific method but the scientists try to solve problems from as many methods as possible and the available evidences show that there are certain definite steps which may be considered and are same in all branches of scientific enquiries. Various steps of scientific investigations are as follows:

1. Observations
2. Forming hypothesis
3. Analysis and synthesis using inductive and deductive approaches
4. Intuitiveness and creativity
5. Drawing inferences
6. Application of knowledge in daily life

The step-wise investigation can be better understood by the following examples:

A teacher in a class has to teach the concept of chair to the class. The teacher first makes the student differentiate chair from other objects by the process of observation, forming hypothesis about a chair, analysing the features of a chair and drawing inferences. The student then applies this knowledge attained by scientific investigation to daily life situations.

The example involves various steps of scientific investigation in which lies the essence of scientific temper which can be followed by anyone and not the scientists alone. Scientific temper is basically an attitude of a person. This has ample relevance for a student in his earlier stage and in later stage of his career.

Scientific temper and its implication for Elementary School Education

To understand implications of scientific temper in elementary school education, one should have a closer look at the school curriculum at the elementary school stage. The school curriculum may be spelled out in terms of—Why? What? When? How? And Through what context?

To achieve the above approach, a well planned structured and flexible elementary school science education programme is the first requisite, and in the same may enable the teachers to deal with difficult classroom situations arising at the local, national and global level.

References

1. Jawahar Lal Nehru, Discovery of India, Bombay: Asia Publishing, 1961.
2. Nehru, op. Cit.
3. Rabindra Nath Tagore, London: Macmillan, 1962, p. 101.
4. Nehru, op. Cit.
5. Hem Lata Singh, Scientific Temper and Education, Commonwealth Publishers, New Delhi, 1990.
6. Nehru op. Cit.
7. Rethinking Science Education, Part-I, National Society for Study of Community Education (Chicago; Univ. of Chicago Press, 1960, p. 35.
8. Science, The Columbia Encyclopaedia, 3rd Edition, 1963, p. 1990.
9. Arthur Carimand Sund B. Robert. Discovery Teaching in Science, Columbia, Ohio: Charles E. Merril Publishing Company, 1966, pp. 4-10.

X

Elementary School Science
Psychological Basis of Learning

> The entire object of true education is to make people not merely to do the right things, but enjoy them; not merely industrious, but to love industry; not merely learned, but to love knowledge; not merely pure, but to love purity; not merely just, but to hunger and thirst after justice.
>
> —*John Ruskin*

Elementary School teachers in the third world countries today face an increasing number of curriculum decisions especially in the area of science education. An avalanche of scientific knowledge has thundered upon man in the last two decades. How can elementary school teachers supply meaningful science education experiences to their pupils with reference to this explosion of knowledge?

The above dilemma suggests an important role that psychology has to play in the learning process in science education especially dealing with the concepts *of Readiness* and *Motivation.*

Coming to the specifics of Readiness, Bruner has aptly written:

> We begin with the hypothesis that any subject can be taught effectively in some intellectually honest form to any child at any stage of development. It is a bold hypothesis and essential in thinking about the nature of a curriculum. No evidence exists to contradict it; considerable evidence is being amassed that supports it.

Research on the intellectual development of the child highlights the fact that at each stage of development, the child has a characteristic way of viewing the world and explaining it to himself. The task of teaching a subject to a child at any particular age is one of representing the structure of that subject in terms of the child's way of viewing things. The task can be thought of as one of translation. The general hypothesis that has just been stated is promised on the considered judgement that any idea can be represented honestly and usefully in the thought forms of children of school age, and that these first representations can later be made more powerful and precise easily by virtue of this early learning[1].

Another important concern for the teacher is the psychological problem in the elementary science of arousing interest in the pupil to learn science. This problem may indicate motivating students to learn science. An emotionally satisfying science education experience is one of the most important reinforcement factors for imparting meaningful and lasting science education experiences to the pupils.

Burner has described about "motivation" in the following paragraph:

> Somewhere between apathy and wild excitement, there is an optimum level of aroused attention that is ideal for class room activity. What is that level? Frenzied activity fostered by the conceptive competitive project may leave no pause for reflection, for evaluation, for generalisation, while excessive orderliness, with each student waiting passively for his turn, produces boredom and ultimate apathy. There is a day-to-day problem here of great significance. Short-term arousal of interest is not the same as the long-term establishment of interests in the broader sense. Films, audio-visual aids, and other such devices may have the effect of catching attention. In the long run, they may produce a passive person waiting for some curtain to group to arouse him[2].

In addition to the above concepts, science teachers must recognise the following generalisation regarding the learning processes and their implications for science education.

Learning—An Acquisition of Knowledge

Generalisation 1

Learning takes place with greater effectiveness when the learner is provided with frequent knowledge of what progress he is making provided such knowledge is given soon after the learning experience.

The subject of learning and reinforcement has been the object of much investigation ever since Thorndike's experiments in 1898. There is much evidence to support the above generalisation. The knowledge of progress does indeed act as reinforcement and this aids in the learning process.

One of the most comprehensive studies made on the influence of knowledge of progress was that of Book and Norvelle[3]. The ability of 124 samples was tested for their ability to make legible "a" and "s". The group with knowledge of progress excelled the other in each of the first ten practice periods but lost its advantage when knowledge of progress was withheld.

The most common classroom device used to give knowledge of progress is tests and quizzes. Standlee and Popham[4] pointed out that quizzes and tests affect student learning by acting as an enforced activity with respect to the subject-matter. Using students philosophy at the college level, Deputy found that with three groups he tested, sections having written tests during the term did significantly better than the sections having no tests but only oral reviews. Hertzberger, Hailman and Leuenberger[5] administered short quizzes to students taking a course in educational psychology each week. After the first five weeks the authors found the group using the objective tests to be superior in achievement. Fitch, Drucker and Norton[6] came to a similar conclusion while testing college students taking a course in government.

There is some research evidence to support the theory that the lower intelligence groups particularly benefit from the reinforcement value of knowledge of progress. After conducting an experiment on knowledge of progress, Fay concluded that "students of low intelligence particularly need to know their marks"[7] Similar observations were made by Kulp[8] and Noll[9] in experiments they conducted.

Studies conducted by Keller and Skinner[10] indicate that there is a definite time relationship between the response and the effect it produces on the learner. Kimble[11] in an experiment found that immediate feedback appears to be necessary for learning to process rapidly.

How frequent should knowledge of success be given? Lewis[12] found that as far as the immediate acquisition of a skill was concerned, 100 per cent reinforcement was desirable. When, however, the learning task is more complex, such a degree of reinforcement may not be necessary and possibly even hinders learning.

Implications for Science Education

According to the evidence cited, the learner needs to have immediate feedback of his progress if learning is to proceed quickly. This principle has been frequently neglected in educational practice and particularly in the evaluation procedures and correction of laboratory notebooks in a science class. Quite often a science teacher will allow such an extended amount of time to elapse between the evaluation and the feedback to the pupil that the effect of knowledge of performance is negligible in facilitating learning.

Tests and lab recordings should be marked and returned to the student as quickly as possible. No doubt, the correcting of the lab notebooks presents a real problem to a science teacher. In the present writer's opinion, the teacher should correct lab notebooks during class time, thus allowing "feedback" to the students.

It is also evident from the research evidence that knowledge of progress given frequently is valuable for reinforcement. Perhaps the brighter pupil will not need to have the knowledge of progress they make, made available to them externally as often as slower students because the brighter students are more capable of internal checking. Studies made by Noll[13] and Fay[14] indicate that lower ability groups particularly benefit from frequent knowledge of progress. A science teacher teaching such groups would be well advised to give knowledge of progress often and after smaller learning steps.

From what is known of reinforcement and knowledge of progress it is evident that a child must be given a curriculum in which he can experience success. A student who experiences repeated failures is likely to give up trying to learn altogether. There may be some value in difficult exercises and examinations but if they result in a repeated failure their value can be questioned. The old saying "nothing succeeds like success" still holds good.

Generalisation 2

Learning proceeds most effectively when the activity or material to be learned is geared to the level of the learner's readiness. Such readiness may be defined as physical maturity, mental age, or the skills or operations required to perform a certain task.

There has been considerable experimentation done on the effect of a child's chronological age and his ability to perform various skills. But since we are concerned here more with the acquisition of knowledge the studies cited to support the generalisation above will be limited to readiness, meaning thereby mental age and what Woody[15] calls "educational readiness."

Fostor[16] showed in an experiment with children between the mental ages of 3 and 5 that the ability to memorise stories improved from mental age 3 to 5. Morphett and Washburne[17] found in studying reading readiness that children with a mental age of 5 could not learn to read whereas children with a mental age of 6–7 made satisfactory progress. Frandsen[18] reports a study Brueckner which showed that mental age was significantly related to progress. In another study, Washburne[19] and his committee found, in extensive investigations, that with increasing mental maturity, a greater percentage of students were able to meet the criterion of satisfactory learning of various skills in arithmetic. Guided by maturation achievement curves, his committee recommended the mental age placements for various arithmetic concepts and skills. Browne[20] found by using diagnostic tests that students were "occasionally ready" to take various tests in arithmetic at different times. This was evidently more a result of previous learning, he contended, than a physiological readiness. Although Gagne[21] did his research in the area of transfer, his studies imply that a pupil is ready for the materials at some given level only if he has attained the learning set up to that level.

Implications for Science Education

It is common sense that academic learning cannot be postponed until the time of maximum learning efficiency. Age may not be the same when science learning proceeds most rapidly, but a start must be made. The science educator must plan a programme so that by the time adulthood is reached, the maximum amount of learning will have taken place. To do this one must begin as early as possible using science curriculum materials that can be understood by the child and progressing to increasing degrees of complexity at a rate commensurate with the mental development of the pupil.

Furthermore, if "educational readiness" is taken into consideration, science teachers will have to make practical judgements about when to introduce new concepts or material. This means that every science teacher will need to have a thorough knowledge of the subject and considerable ability ascertaining the readiness of each pupil to undertake new learning. This will necessitate grouping and much individualised instruction so that new materials are presented in such a way that the pupil will be able to cope with it. Thus, while teaching elementary science much emphasis should be laid on the physical and natural sciences concerning the environment.

Our present system of grade placement of students, although based to an extent on the idea of maturation level, in effect hinders the application of what might be learned from research. Chronological age and mental age do not always correspond, and thus many pupils who are taught in the same class by the same methods and using the same instructional material are either not ready to understand the material or are ready to advance to more complex forms of learning but are prevented from doing so by their grade placement.

Thus, if learning is geared to the maturation level, desirable outcomes should result. Satisfaction will come from success and interest will increase. Because of the success, the learner will become more self-confident and attack with greater effectiveness a wide variety of problems

Retention and Forgetting

Generalisation 1

Repetition beyond the criterion of initial correctness is necessary to ensure maximum retention of materials learned.

Benton J. Underwood, states in the Scientific American that the "ultimate degree of learning rather than the rate of learning is the critical factor in forgetting."[22] Many studies have indicated that one of the basic aims of education, retention, is aided by over-learning.

Much of the interest in forgetting and retention shown by researchers in this century was inspired by the work of Hermann Ebbinghaus.[23] He found that a series of syllables which were learned twice faded away more slowly than those that were learned only once. More often they were repeated the less easily they were forgotten. Kreuger[24] used a list of 12 monosyllabic nouns on a memory drum to find whether increased learning was proportional to retention. He concluded that "a certain degree of over-learning, at least 50 per cent, is highly economical from the standpoint of retention for intervals of 2 to 28 days, and the larger the interval the greater the conomy."[25]

Klausmeier and Check,[26] however, put little faith in trying to draw conclusions for understanding retention of classroom learning of meaningless syllables. It may be well, therefore, to cite experiments conducted under classroom conditions. Spitzer[27] made a study of the effect of recall tests on retention. He found that they were effective methods of aiding retention since the students reviewed the material learned. Raffel[28] studied the effect of recall on learning words by college students. She found that retention tests given at spaced intervals acted as relearning devices and were superior to other schedules of testing.

Other investigations have attempted to ascertain the effect of review on retention. Peterson[29] and others investigated the effect of review of historical materials on retention in college classes. One review group showed a superiority of 57 per cent over the control group. Tiedman[30] found that retention of material learned in the classroom was significantly benefitted by review tests.

Implications for Science Education

Science teachers for many years have been familiar with the fact that one of the best ways to prevent subsequent forgetting is to provide for over-learning. But mere repetition does not guarantee that what is to be learned will be more easily retained. To make one repeat 100 times any scientific principle does not guarantee that he has learned. In fact it may well work the other way. The repetition or review must be meaningful to the pupil and he must want to retain. The science teacher, therefore, should device methods that will keep the review from merely taking the form of drill or rote learning. This can be done in numerous ways. A pupil may learn a concept in science but instead of his repeating it over and over it would be well to utilise the skill in the solution of problems in a large number of different circumstances so that ample opportunity is provided for over learning. Recall tests, reviews and exercises can be used frequently and varied frequently to save the learner from becoming bored, and yet providing for over learning.

Generalisation 2

If there is a failure of recall, it is probably because of the interference coming from subsequent new learning. However, subsequent new learning need not necessarily mean that there will be failure in recall.

There has been a considerable amount of research done on "interference theory" or "retroactive inhibition". Since there are numerous variables to be considered in experiments on retroactive inhibition and forgetting, most of the investigators consider one or more of these variables as part of their study. Mordock[31] has demonstrated that interference among verbal items can be shown with chains as short as three variable item if a learner is instructed to count backwards by three's from some given number. McGeoch[32] found that retroactive inhibition was partly a function of the number of repetitions of interpolated lists. The same authors[33] also found the synonymity between the members of the original and interpolated lists to be a highly favourable condition for the production of retroactive inhibition, and hence forgetting.

Melton and Irwin[34] have found that using 5,10,20 and 40 trials for the interpolated learning of 18 nonsense syllables, the greatest retroactive inhibition occurred after ten trial interpolations, and the least for five. In another experiment, Melton and Lackum[35] demonstrated that part of the total interference must be attributed to factors other than competition at the point of recall. They identified another factor as the unlearning of the original response.

Osgood, in one study, agreed that interference was because of forgetting but denied the general belief that "the greater the similarity the greater the retroactive interference" has general validity.[36] This however, as Bugelski[37] points out, may be because the problem of defining "similarity" has never been solved satisfactorily.

Implications for Science Education

One of the obvious conclusions one could draw from the research evidence is that if new scientific principle interferes with old learning and causes a failure of recall, then there is little point in learning things that will interfere but the old saying "the more I learn the more I forget" is not entirely true; this can be overcome in a number of ways.

One of the ways to overcome interference is to over-learn the material to be learned and, as already pointed out, make it more resistant to forgetting. If a science teacher is aware of the fact of interference, he can make sure that the material is thoroughly learned before new learning is introduced.

Another way of combating retroactive inhibition is for the science teacher to be constantly teaching science with discrimination in mind. For example, the present writer has found it worthwhile to help pupils distinguish thoroughly between some of the similar scientific concepts.

It has also been shown by research that if the material is meaningful to the learner, it is less easily forgotten and less easily interfered with. Science teachers, therefore, should attempt to make the learning experiences of the pupil as meaningful as possible through careful motivation and application to real life.

Thus the teaching of science has a number of purposes to achieve if it is to merit a place in the school curriculum.

It should carry young pupils further along in their understanding of selected generalised concepts, the methods of science, and social implications of science. It should develop an appreciation of the role of science in advancing man's understanding and control of the world of nature. It should develop a disposition to use the knowledge and methods of science whenever appropriate. It should develop abilities that make young people increasingly independent investigators and learners.[38]

Transfer of Training

Generalisation 1

The greatest degree of transfer occurs in the learning of principles and generalisations that have many applications rather than isolated learning of facts.

The theory of transfer emphasising the importance of grasping broad meaning and principles and of organising and generalising one's particular experiences has been sponsored chiefly by Charles H. Judd and his followers. He found in his classic experiment using boys trying to hit an under-water target that theory with practice is a great asset[39]. The classic experiment of Judd was to some extent redone by Hendridickson and Schroeder[40] who concluded that transfer was likely to be most effective when based on a grasp of common principles, formulae or rules. Begely[41] reports in "The Educative Process" that in one experiment where a teacher emphasised neatness in arithmetic only and not in other subjects, no transfer occurred. This same experiment was done by Reudiger[42] with the variation that the teacher stressed neatness as an ideal to be used at home and school, the result was that students exhibited greater neatness in all school subjects.

Research studies show that there is considerable transfer value in instructing towards generalising and formulation of various principles of rules. Overman,[43] for instance, found significant gains in arithmetic for the group that had practice only. Breed[44] found that realisation and generalisation was even useful for transfer in teaching spellings. Olander[45] showed that learning more isolated facts did not facilitate transfer. He found that in teaching a Group of 200 number there was no more transfer than for the group that studied only 110 combinations.

Implications for Science Education

Research evidence points to the advantage of formulating operational definitions, principles or rules. The more broadly based the definition, principle or rule, the better will be its chance of transfer to new and different situations. Accordingly the usefulness of any principle, etc., will be increased if it is practised in as wide a variety of circumstances as possible.

"Learning set" has been defined by Gagne as "knowledge relevant to any given final task to be learned" or a set of subordinate capabilities."[46] A considerable amount of Gagne's research was aimed at a study of "learning sets" and transfer of training. In one of his experiments using ninth grade Algebra students, he found that success at higher levels was dependent upon the attainment of learning sets at the next lower level.[47]

It has been shown by several investigation that it is possible to develop a general "set" towards learning which results in learning how to learn. This has been shown quite dramatically by Harlow and Warren[48] in their experiment with a monkey learning to solve a series of mechanical puzzles. After much trouble with the first task, thc monkey developed a general approach or "set that assisted him to learn succeeding similar task much more quickly". Reed,[49] using college students as subjects, found in his experiment that the groups of students who had included in their preparation for the task a set to employ meaningful concepts learned the tasks more efficiently than the group not thus prepared.

Provision needs to be made by the teacher to encourage the pupils to apply learnt principles widely and in as great a variety of situations as possible. If, for instance, the science teacher was teaching the principle of the "balance of nature" it would be well to introduce living examples into the classroom or perhaps to go on a field trip and observe first hand. If the teacher gives guidance in the application of principles, the more able pupil will probably be able to find a wide variety of applications on his own. For the less able pupil, such guidance may result in some specific rules of thumbs such as "It is deeper than it looks" whereas the general principles may not have registered at all.

It is only these principles or generalisations which are adequately grasped are likely to prove useful in transfer. For this reason, more transfer may be obtained from a simple elegant rule which a pupil grasps rather than a complicated definition that he can repeat but does not understand. Science teachers should be careful to take into account the intellectual levels of the pupils since it is obvious that the brighter pupil will be able to handle more theoretical principles and ideas than the less able who will only be confused with complicated terminology.

Generalisation 2

The learning of principles and generalisations results in the emergence of a "learning set" which, in effect, permits the learner to go on to the next learning step and thus facilitates transfer.

Siegel[50] in a recent experiment made a strong case for altering the educational set in a conceptual direction.

Implications for Science Education

The results of the experiments cited indicate the necessity of building "Learning sets" in pupils so that learned knowledge will have the greatest possible transfer. This can be done in a number of ways. The science teacher should teach his pupils to be alert for the application of principles learned. The pupil should be taught to tackle new problems without any hesitation. A general habit should be developed, which has often been rewarded, of looking for further applications of principles and generalisations. It follows that such a habit will develop best in an integrated curriculum arranged in sequences and with provision for the application of old and new principles continuously. If, for instance, the pupil has been taught in science to make generalisations from being taught critical thinking, the science teacher could apply these generalisations by having quoted in current scientific achievements. Gradually the pupil should come up and make applications of his own. In other words, he will have learned how to learn.

The above generalisations concerning learning processes have lot of ramifications for evaluation of science education experience at the elementary level.

References

1 Jerome S. Butrner, The Process of Education, Harvard Univ. Press, 1960, p.33

2 Ibid.

3 W.F. Book, L. Norvell, "An Experimental Study of Learning Incentives", Pedagogical Seminar XXIX, (December, 1922), pp. 305-362.

4 Lloyd S. Standlee, W.J. Popham, "Quizzes Contribution to Learning," Journal of Educational Psychology, L1. (December, 1960), pp. 322-325.

5 O.E. Hertzberger, J.D. Heilman, W.D. Leuenberger, the Value of Objective Tests as Teaching Devices", Journal of Educational Psychology, XXIII, (May, 1932)) pp. 371-380.

6 W.L. Fitch A.J. Drucker, J.A. Norton, "Frequent Testing as a Motivating Factor in large Lecture Classes", Journal of Educational Psychology, XIII, (January, 1951) pp. 1-20.

7 P.J. Fay, "The Effect of the Knowledge of Results on Subsequent Achievement of College Students, "Journal of Educational Psychology, XXVIII, (October, 1937), pp. 548-554.

8 D.H. Kulp, "Weekly Tests for Graduate Students", Schools and Society, XXXVIII, (July 1933), pp. 157-159.

9 V.H. Noll, "The Effect of Written Tests upon Achievement in College Courses : An Experiment and Summary of Evidence", Journal of Educational Research, XXXII, (January, 1939) pp.345-358.

10 R.M. Gagne. The Conditions of Learning, New York: Holt, Rinehart and Winston, Inc., 1965), p. 224.

11 P.M. Symonds, What Education has to Learn from Psychology, (Columbia University : Bureau of Publication, 1964), p.17.

12 J.M. Stephens, The Psychology of classroom Learning, New York: Holt, Reinehart & Co., 1965), p.215.

13 Noll, op. cit., pp. 345-358.

14 Fay, op. cit., pp. 548-554.

15 F.T. Tyler, "Issues Related to Readiness to Learn, "National Society for the Study of Edu, IXIII, Part I, (Chicago: University of Chicago Press, 1964), p-220.(Woody)

16 A.N. Frandsen, How Children Learn, (New York. McGraw. Hill Blook Co., 1957), p.74

17 Ibid, p.75

18 A.N. Frandsen, How children learn, (New York: McGraw. Hill Book Co., 1957), p.76

19 Ibid., pp.77-79

20 Tyler, loc. cit (Browne)

21 Tyler, op. cit., pp.228-229 (Gagne)

22 Benton, J Underwood, "Forgetting", Scientific American, CCX, (March, 1964), p.92.

23 Hermann Ebbinghaus, Memory—A Contribution to Experimental Psychology, Trans, by H.A. Ruger and C.E. Bussenius, (New York: Dover Publications Inc., 1964). P.81.

24 W.C. Krueger, "The Effect of Overlearning on Retention"., Journal of Experimental Psychology XII, (December, 1929), p.78.

25 Ibid., p. 71

26 H.J. Klausmeier, J. Check, "Retention and Transfer in Children of Low, Average and High Intelligence", Journal of Educational Research, LV. (April 1962), pp. 319-322.

[27] H.F. Spitzer, "Studies in Retention", Journal of Educational Psychology, XXX, (December 1939. P.655.

[28] G. Raffel, "The Effect of Recall on Forgetting", Journal of Experimental Psychology, XVI, (December 1934), 828-838.

[29] H.A. Peterson, M. Ellis, N. Tohill, P. Kloess, "Some Measurements of the Effects of Reviews", Journal of Educational Psychology, XXV, (1935), pp. 65-72.

[30] H.R. Tiedman, "A Study in the Retention of Classroom Learning", Journal of Educational Research, XLI, (March 1948), pp.516-531.

[31] B.B. Mordock, "The Retention of Individual Items", Journal of Experimental psychology. PLXII, (1961), pp. 618-625.

[32] J.A. McGeoch, G. McGeoch, "The Influence of Degree of Interpolated Learning on Retroactive Inhibition", American Journal of Psychology, XLIV, (1932) 695-708.

[33] McGeoch, "Studies in Retroactive Inhibition, VI: The Influence of the relative Serial Positions of Interpolated Synonyms", Journal of Experimental Psychology, XIX, (1936), pp. 1-23.

[34] A.W. Melton, J.M. Irwin, "The Influence of Degree of Interpolated Learning on Retroactive Inhibition and the Overt Transfer of Specific Responses," American Journal of Psychology, LIII, (1940), pp. 173-203.

[35] A.M. Melton, W.J. Lackum, "Retroactive and Proactive Inhibition in Retention: Evidence for a Two Factor Theory of Retroactive Inhibition," American Journal of Psychology, LIV, (1941), pp. 157-173

[36] C.E. Osgood, "An Investigation into the Cause of Retroactive interference." Journal of Psychology, XXXVIII, (1948), pp. 132-154.

[37] B.R. Bugelski, The Psychology of Learning, (New York: Henry Holt & Co., 1956), p.321.

[38] Robert H. Carleton, Improving Secondary School Science from Rethinking Science Education, The 59th Yearbook of the National Society of Education, Part I, University of Chicago, 1960.

[39] Frandsen, op, cit., pp.135-187.

[40] Ibid., p.186

[41] H. Woodrow, "The Effect of Type of Training Upon Transference," Journal of Educational Psychology, XVIII, (1927). pp. 159-171.

[42] W.C. Reudiger, "Indirect Improvement of Mental Functions through Ideals," Educational Review, XXXVI, (1908), pp. 364-371.

[43] J.K. Overman, "An Experimental Study of the Effect of the method of Instructions on Transfer of Training in Arithmetic." "Elementary School Journal XXXL. (1930), pp.183-190.

[44] F.S. Breed, "Generalisation in Spelling," Elementary School Journal, XXXVI, (1937), pp. 733-741.

45 H.T. Olander, "Transfer of Training in Simple Addition and Subtraction," Elementary School Journal, XXXI, (1931), pp. 427-437.

46 Tyler, op. cit., pp. 230-231.

47 Tyler, op. cit., p.231

48 Stephens, op. cit., p.215.

49 H.B. Reed, Factors Influencing Learning and Retention of Concepts, I: The Influence of Set, "Journal of Experimental Psychology, XXXVI, (1946), 71-87.

50 L. Siegel, L. Siegel, "Education Set, "A Determinant of Acquisition", Journal of Educational Psychology, LVI, (February, 1965). pp. 1-12.

XI

Evaluating Science Education
Based on Environmental and Integrated Approach

NPE has aptly made the following observations concerning Elementary Education, Science Education and the Evaluation Process and Examination Reform.

Para 5.5 Elementary Education

The new thrust in elementary education will emphasise two aspects: (i) universal enrolment and universal retention of children up to 14 years of age, and (ii) a substantial improvement in the quality of education.

Para 8.18 Science Education

Science education will be strengthened so as to develop in the child well defined abilities and values such as the spirit of enquiry, creativity, objectivity, courage to question and an aesthetic sensibility.

Para 8.19 Science education programmes will be designed to enable the learner to acquire problem solving and decision-making skills and to discover the relationship of science with health, agriculture, industry and other aspects of daily life. Every effort will be made to extend science education to the vast numbers who have remained outside the pale of formal education.

The Evaluation Process and Examination Reform

Para 8.23 Assessment of performance is an integral part of any process of learning and teaching. As part of sound educational strategy, examinations should be employed to bring about qualitative improvements in education.

Para 8.24 The objectives will be to re-cast the examination system so as to ensure a method of assessment that is a valid and reliable measure of student development and a powerful instrument for improving teaching and learning. In functional terms, this would mean:

1. The elimination of excessive element of chance and subjectivity;

2. The dė-emphasis of memorisation;
3. Continuous and comprehensive evaluation that incorporates both scholastic and non-scholastic aspects of education, spread over the total span of instructional time;
4. Effective use of the evaluation process by teachers, students and parents;
5. Improvement in the conduct of examinations;
6. Introduction of the semester system from the secondary stage in a phased manner; and
7. The use of grades in place of marks.
8 The introduction of concomitant changes in instructional materials and methodology.

It is gratifying to note that the above significant curricular improvements in science education have been made in India. There have been some major improvements in the area of evaluation (examination) also.

Status of Evaluation and Examination System in India —An Introspection

The system of examination and evaluation in India, generally reflects the existing system of education. At present, teaching and learning are primarily done for the purpose of passing the examinations. The traditional science curriculum especially at the secondary and senior secondary levels in India in fact places emphasis on memorisation of certain principles. Teachers are expected to follow closely the syllabus prescribed by the stage, and the curriculum are such as to enforce a descriptive and didactic process of teaching. The teacher feels that he will be branded "poor" if he does not complete the prescribed course within the term. Furthermore, his competence is judged by the percentage of students passing the departmental or university examinations.

The above conviction is substantiated by the Education Commission (1964-66) in the following paragraph.

"Perhaps the greatest evil from which school, university, and college education in India suffers is that teaching is thus subordinated to examination rather than examination serving to facilitate teaching".[1]

The above conviction is also supported in the following observation by Bloom of the University of Chicago:

Examinations do much to control the behaviour, thoughts and attitudes of students and teachers alike. But no living individual or group is in control over the examinations, only a body of traditions and practices which have accumulated over the years. The syllabus usually contains a detailed list of topics and it suggests that education is equated with the acquisition of some detailed information on each of the topics listed. The effect of such a syllabus and the pressure of time and numbers of students make information on each topic the major objective emphasised by the examiner and cramming of such information is the major task undertaken by the student.

A comparison of the question papers over several years reveals a highly stereotyped character in the questions set. Originality in setting questions is not valued. The necessary materials for setting a paper include the syllabus, the old question papers, and some tools as the student used in his preparation for the examination.[2]

From the financial as well as from the academic standpoints, it seems highly undesirable to subjects the pupils' work of a full year, or more, to a single externally formulated examination as the sole basis for evaluating progress. Superintendents, invigilators, and supervisors are hired at each examinations centre, adding to the cost of maintaining the examination system. The money spent on these external examinations might be better utilised in improving the existing facilities in educational institutions.

Further, in a survey by Cormack, author of the Rides a Peacock Indian Students and Social Change, Indian Students objected to the following aspects of the educational system in India:

1. The external examinations,
2. Insufficient choice in selecting course,
3. Not being allowed to express their ideas freely,
4. The aloofness of teachers.

In summary, the examination system represents a drawback in the educational system of India in general.

Examinations and the Threat of Failure

Generally, failures result in frustration implying, to a certain extent, that education is a painful process. Education should be more a source of pleasure to the student than a source of pain, instilling in him a desire to learn, reinforced by guidance from a qualified, interested and humane teacher. This does not necessarily mean to make education easier, however. It means, rather, that the role of the threat of failure should be reduced and that of motivation increased. The threat of failure has negative effect on the pupil, the threat results in a dislike for the subject. On the other hand, success is more likely to result when interest is aroused. The development of interest, motivating the students to do quality work should be the responsibility of the teacher. Clearly, teachers should increase their attempts to motivate pupils by making their teaching more interesting and meaningful. Teaching aimed solely at passing the external examination is not likely to be either interesting or meaningful in science education especially at the elementary level.

Coming to the specifics of technology/methods of teaching science at the elementary level, it is desired to explore some ways in which the examination system can be adapted so as to reduce the level of threat and, hopefully, to provide more opportunities for development of a higher level of understanding than that reflected by rote memory. As a first step, it seems to be necessary to remove the all-or-nothing concept in which the external examinations operate. To implement the concept of continuous and comprehensive evaluation, the focus of examination should not be only on the performance of a student in written examination but also on the transference of scientific knowledge to daily life situations and development of scientific attitude and scientific behaviour. The following Schematic Representation No. I provides a record keeping device for meaningful evaluation of science at the elementary level.

The above conviction suggests that before relegating a student to a poor grading *i.e.*, a "third division" or a "D" grade for poor performance, especially in the "one-try" sink or swim" nature of the external examination (as practised at the secondary or senior secondary level), the teacher should have exercised planned series of evaluative steps aimed at integrating evaluation with teaching so that it not only provides feedback on attainment but also serves as an important teaching tool.

Schematic Representation No. II suggests an evaluation sequence recognising different degrees of background and science proficiency based on environmental and integrated approach to science education.

Statement showing the Evaluation of Student in Science at the Elementary Level

Please tick (✓) the appropriate response

S. No.	Criteria	*Unit-I (Ch. I, II, III)*				*Unit-II (Ch. VI, V)*				*Unit-III (Ch. VI, VII)*				*Unit-IV (Ch. VIII, IX)*				*Comments*
		E	*G*	*S*	*U*	*E*	*G*	*S*	*U*	*E*	*G*	*S*	*U*	*E*	*G*	*S*	*U*	
1.	General understanding of the concepts																	
2.	Expresses ideas in terms of scientific language																	
3.	Observation power																	
4.	Forming hypothesis																	
5.	Drawing inferences																	
6.	Interpreting data																	
7.	Experimenting and manipulative skills																	
8.	Ability to express ideas clearly																	
9.	Active participation in the class discussion																	
10.	Original approach to the course																	
11.	Application of knowledge to the daily life																	
12.	Home assignments																	
13.	Behaviour change																	

E—Excellent; G—Good; S—Satisfactory; U—Unsatisfactory

Schematic Representation No. 1

An Evaluation Sequence which recognises Different Degrees of Background and Science Proficiency Based on Environment

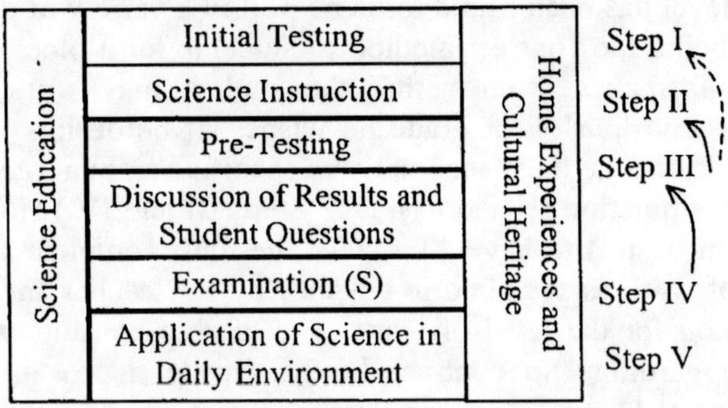

Schematic Representation No. 2

The evaluation model suggested in Schematic II comprises the following steps.

Step I: Initial Testing

Initial tests are designed to reveal the previous level of achievement in a particular area of elementary science. These are thus diagnostic in nature. If the teacher is aware of the background of his students, he should be able to develop an individualised or semi-individualised programme of studies designed to correct background deficiencies and meet instructional goals according to the needs of the student, while maintaining a pace designed to allow the better students to complete a significant amount of work.

Step II: Instruction

As discussed earlier regarding the threat of failure, the writer believes that the mode of instruction can be adapted so as to reduce the level of threat, with the result that the students are given an increased sense of accomplishment and responsibility. While the purpose of this chapter is not a discussion of instructional method, a brief mention seems appropriate here.

Contract Method and Elementary Science Education

In order to accomplish the aim indicated above, the author feels that the single, whole-class methodology must be modified to allow for varying degrees of individualisation of the work. As an example of a useful mode of individualisation, the contract method at the upper primary level has been found to be helpful in a variety of situations. In introducing the contract method to students for a block of work, the teacher makes it clear that the student may work towards obtaining any division or grade he wishes. If he desires to have a "third division", he must accomplish a specified amount of work and pass an examination related to it (see Steps III and IV.) However, if the student desires to have "A grade", he must complete additional amount of work as specified in advance by the teacher and pass the examination for the level of work. The teacher consults with each student regarding the contract he has made as to its realistic probability of being completed. Having agreed on the contract, the student is assured that he will receive the desired grade if he completes the work.

The contract system is a flexible device that can be open ended. For example, if a student feels that he is unable to fulfill that contract, it can be negotiated again. In this mode of learning, the student can feel free to question or to differ with the teacher without fear of its affecting his grade. Class discussions can be more open, encouraging leading to increased level of class participation and generating an atmosphere of freedom in the classroom.

Step III: Pre-Testing

After a programme of instruction in some topic or block of work in elementary science, the instructor should give a pre-test. The "pre" in this usage connote preliminary, an evaluation device not intended to produce grades for record but rather a combined review device and evaluation of the degree to which the material has been understood by the students so that any necessary re-teaching can take place. Further, the students should be asked at this point to develop and submit the questions for discussion and particularly those, which they feel might be used for quizzes (The ability to ask good questions is a useful index of understanding). These questions and the students' participation in discussion of them and of the results of the pre-test should be considered a part of the evaluation for which a place is provided in Schematic II. This discussion and probing via student questions may constitute the needed re-teaching, or some more formal procedures may be prescribed by the teacher.

Step IV: Examination(s)

The next step is the examination. The "examination" could be a single formal-type examination or could consist of a number of quizzes on parts of the topic or block of work. The students should be given a quiz on each major topic or textbook chapter. In order to move on the subsequent topic or chapter, the student must pass the quiz on the current topic or chapter. Each teacher should decide what is a "passing grade". Students should be permitted to take a quiz or a parallel form of it more than once if necessary in the teacher's judgement to move on, but only after some further instruction. (Re-taking of quizzes should be minimised, however, by the use of the pre-test. Some reasonable time limit should be set on how long a student spends on one topic with the teacher exercising judgement as to the continued study.

After passing a quiz or examination, the student returns to step I or II, as needed, and the process repeats. This is "Re-cycling" indicated on the schematic. In some cases, the quiz or examination can serve as the diagnostic initial testing for the next topic and the recycling goes to Step II instead of Step I. Another re-cycling arrow in the schematic indicates the return to Step II from Step III if the pre-test suggests more instruction is necessary.

Step V—Application of Science in Daily Life Environment

This step will bring the school closer to community implying that education, especially science instruction, is a process by which an individual is able to adjust to the needs of the fact changing sociological, psychological and economic pattern of the work-oriented society. Society determines the nature of education and science education can be an instrument for social development.

Also, this step *i.e.*, application of science in daily life environment may be quite conducive for providing meaningful science education experiences in environmental and integrated approach to science teaching as envisaged in the National Policy on Education (1986)

The evaluation system in elementary science education should foster development of a positive self-concept for each student. It is quite common that poor students' failure, especially in rural schools, is due to unhealthy perceptions of the self and the world. Evaluation procedures must recognise the right of the child to be appreciated for what he is and for what he has the potential to become. The writer has already suggested a method of evaluation that he felt will impart a reasonable feeling of possible success to these students, through a reduced level of emphasis on one-try evaluation of rote-learned material. This method is also in consonance with the concept of continuous and comprehensive evaluation.

This method of integrating evaluation with teaching also takes into consideration the likelihood that some of the better students may complete any given examination in less than the prescribed time limit. To satisfy these more rapid learners, the teacher should provide differential assignments involving more difficult task and evaluations, probably leading to first or high second division (A or B grades).

Some Suggestions regarding Improving the Evaluation System in Environmental Studies.

The following suggestions are felt to be generally desirable, rather than absolutely necessary to the teaching environment. It should be kept in mind that these suggestions are not meant to be prescriptive nor are they necessarily applicable in all situation.

1. Evaluation procedures should be consistent with the philosophy of continuous growth. The problem of external examinations is not simply the presence of examinations themselves, but the degree to which they dominate the entire system of evaluation. To measure progress, we must evaluate each student against himself by taking into consideration his present level and his past level of achievement as well as that of others.
2. An effort should be made to devise an individualised programme for each student at the elementary level. The writer has suggested a method of valuation which incorporates the concept of individualisation (refer to Schematic Representation No. II). The evaluation system should be organised to permit some greater degree of flexibility. A rigid external examination with emphasis on memorisation is not in accord with our present.
3. Evaluation in Elementary Science should put stress on (I) helping pupils learn to think, (ii) to develop fresh meanings for themselves, (iii) to examine possibilities and to create new

combinations from original or available data. That is to say, evaluation should be, itself, an act of teaching.

4. Students should be given opportunities to develop the concept of self-evaluation. The pupils should be encouraged and assisted in setting achievable goals for themselves. What is the use of teachers' establishing lofty goals for their students if they are incapable of achieving them? The resulting frustration adds to the problem of low self-concept. The students should be encouraged to participate in class and groups discussions. The participation in group discussions would help each student to know his responsibility in a group situation and become aware of his own strengths and weaknesses.

5. Evaluation in elementary science should not be confined to school buildings. Field trips should be an integral part of the school programme. The students should be encouraged to utilise community facilities. The following example illustrates the idea:

   Rather than giving the written essay-type examination on the topic "Applications of Science in our Lives", totally within the classroom, the students should be asked to submit a report on the above topic by making use of community resources (*Panchayat* Officer, parents and other learned community members).

6. The broad aim of elementary science should be to develop in students the ability to work with the materials of their environment and to solve problems presented to them. Thus the evaluation system should not only focus on the performance of a student in written examination but also on the development of positive scientific attitudes and scientific behaviour (refer to Schematic Representation No. 1).

7. Another most important aspect of evaluation is questioning technique. Questioning is indeed a very challenging technique. In order to be expert in this technique, one has to know not only the subject matter but also a good deal of psychology. The writer suggests a concerted effort within the existing system to upgrade the average teachers' skills in questioning technique which is essential to increase in the teachers' role in the evaluation system.

References

1. R.M. Kalra, "The Chemistry Teacher in a Developing Country", The Journal of Canadian Chemical Education, October, 1969), pp. 5-6.
2 Report of the Education Commission (1964-66), (New Delhi: Government of India Publication, 1966) p.162.
3 Benjamin Bloom, Evaluation in Secondary Schools, Delhi: DEPSE Secondary Education, 1971, p.123

XII

Classroom Research in Science Education
Action Research

Science teachers today face an increasing number of curriculum decisions. An avalanche of scientific knowledge has thundered upon in the last two decades. How can Science teachers supply meaningful educational experiences for children with reference to explosion in scientific knowledge?

It is this writer's belief that recent approaches or trends in Science education, especially at the elementary level, have not made significant changes in actual classroom teaching. It is generally felt that science teachers are not involved in the process of innovations **or** research in science education especially at the elementary level.

The following question arise in one's mind; Can teachers be involved in science education at the elementary level for change in the course content so as to meet gainfully the needs of their students, their communities, and their society?

The response to the above query is positive but difficult. For without involvement all research on classroom processes, those who conducted change cannot come about. It is also believed that the teachers are not competent to this personal type of research that can lead to useful changes in what is taught.

Generally teachers are expected to follow the required syllabus prescribed by the Department of Education, giving teachers limited opportunity to experiment and to try innovate ideas. The present centralised system of education does not encourage to provide quality of science education which the people of each local community desire and need.

Classroom Research in Ancient and Modern India

Concept of action research is very much existent for over the long history of educational system of India. In the Aryan period, the "*Gurukulas*" or "*Ashrams*" correspond to the present day modern colleges. These early institutions were run by individual Gurus. Curriculum and Instruction at the *Gurukulas* was the responsibility of the teacher or Gurus. They determined what the curriculum should be for their pupils. Experts in the fields of mathematics, philosophy, religion and warfare were brought into the *Ashram* to enrich the regular curriculum. Many universities of international repute such as the university of Peshawar (*Purushapura*), *Takshashila* were established where the teachers were responsible for curriculum and instruction, *i.e.*, action research in education was given due importance.

During the time of British rule, the system of education was geared to theoretical knowledge. This has continued with us until the present up to a certain extent.

After independence, in 1947 a philosophy of education advocated by Mahatma Gandhi was based on the fact that the process of education should centre around some form of manual and productive work and that the curriculum should be related to the economics of community structure. The type of education he advocated was aimed at rural reconstruction.

At present, in India we are implementing 10+2+3 pattern of education which intends to prepare children for life education suited to their environment. It is really gratifying to note the above progress in our educational system but it has some ramifications for teacher education. To achieve success in the above pattern of schooling, teacher's role is of utmost importance.

The society in general is dynamic. Rapid social, economic and scientific changes are taking place. If we want to impart meaningful education to our children, teachers must be involved in research, especially in science education, the results of which can have considerable impact on science teaching in the classroom.

Our science teachers, therefore, must be encouraged and given freedom to make many of their own decisions based on the findings

of their research (so-called "Action research"), about the process and content of science teaching. In doing so, science teachers must be encouraged to fulfill their role as professional educators. Also they should be urged to plan and organise work with colleagues and devise new methods of instruction. If science teachers are to profit from their own research activities in science education, they must become familiar with the techniques used in action research. They must be proud of their own research.

Definition of Classroom Research (Action Research)

The activities of science teacher involved in defining and finding solutions to the problems of his classroom is called action research in science education. Action research in science education also may be defined as testing by teachers of experience, process or materials in their classroom. Stephen Corey, a proponent of action research, defines it as a search undertaken by education in the field in order to improve their practices.

Thus, action research in science education is a systematised evaluation of the teacher's own problems in actual classroom teaching. These teachers study their own methods and if we want that the teachers should play an effective role, they should be involved in decision making processes such as curriculum development, and innovations in education etc. To accomplish this, teachers should be given training and responsibility for curriculum and instruction and for action research.

Criticism of Classroom Research

It is often said that teachers in India or in the third world countries are not competent to do action research as they lack knowledge of fundamental research techniques. Moreover, they do not have the time or initiative or interest as they are exhausted during their day's work. Also, lack of money or funds would hinder them to participate in any kind of research. There may be some truth in these claims for teachers all over the world. But action research does not require any special research techniques or special funds. It really does not require much time outside the normal teaching routine. Action research is nothing but the "finding of solution to problems" by teachers in their classes.

How to start Classroom Research?

The following are some steps which may be followed for conducting action research in their own classroom.

Defining a Problem

The first step in a conducting action research is to define a problem which a teacher is having in his classroom. Problems arise out of problematic situations. Suppose some students do not like science. But these students are very much interested in other subjects. Thus, the teacher thinks that there is something wrong, *i.e.*, each student does not like the subject of Environment Studies. The problem here stated prompts the teacher to conduct action research. The problem must be defined clearly. Only if the teacher is fully aware about the problem, then will he be successful in his research.

Step I:

To deal with this problem, the following questions may be considered.

1. Are changes in the science curriculum truly needed?
2. If so, what type of changes are needed?
3. To what extent should science programme be organised to meet the objectives of solving community and personal problems (Practical knowledge in science *i.e.*, work experience activities)?
4. What types of science education activities will prepare students to deal most effectively with personal and community problem?
5. Can I (the teacher) utilise traditional science courses to some extent applying it to the solution of community problems?

Step II: Dealing with the Problem

After the problem is clearly stated it is almost essential to obtain the best evidence to prove that the new methods or materials or strategies developed actually result in the anticipated goals. For example, referring back to the example of unmotivated students, some motivational strátegies like frequent reinforcement techniques may help the students to take more interest in the class. And once some concrete evidence is developed, that must be interpreted.

Step III : Final Step

Thus, the final step in the action research is to interrupt the evidence collected to evaluate the modification made.

An Example of Action Research in Science Education

Problem

What changes should be made in science courses so as to meet the needs of the local community?

The concept of action research is also to provide scientific literacy and ability to apply that knowledge in life situations which they have acquired in actual classroom teaching.

The writer believes that a sincere effort must be made to encourage our teachers to experiment; to devise new ideas for their classroom and to test their ideas.

This is action research in action.